Over the Moon

COMPLETE PRIMARY ENGLISH LANGUAGE PROGRAMME

CU00860140

Shoot for the Stars

4th CLASS Reader

LORRAINE LAWRANCE

GILL EDUCATION

Gill Education
Hume Avenue
Park West
Dublin 12
www.gilleducation.ie

Gill Education is an imprint of M.H. Gill & Co.

ISBN: 978-0-7171-85924

Editor: Caitriona Clarke
Design and layout: Síofra Murphy
Illustrations: Charlie Alder, Oliver Averill, Michael Garton, Katie Kear, Tika and Tata/The Bright Agency

For permission to reproduce photographs, the authors and publisher gratefully acknowledge the following:

© Alamy: 20BC, 66TR, 67, 68, 69, 71T, 75, 83BC, 84CR, 85BR, 90, 127; © DepositPhotos: 47CR; © Flossie Donnelly: 77, 78; © iStock: 18L, 18R, 20TL, 20TC, 20TR, 20BL, 20BR, 21T, 21B, 22, 23L, 23R, 31, 47TL, 47CL, 47BL, 47TR, 47BR, 58, 62, 66BR, 76L, 82TL, 82TC, 82TR, 82CR, 83CR, 83BL, 83BR, 84TR, 85TR, 85CR, 86, 87, 92TR, 92CR, 92BR, 93CR, 94TR, 94CR, 103; © Shutterstock: 71C, 82BR, 93BR; © Sky Rota: 74, 76R.

The paper used in this book is made from the wood pulp of managed forests. For every tree felled, at least one tree is planted, thereby renewing natural resources.

The authors and publisher are grateful to the following for permission to reproduce copyrighted material:

'When You Thought I Wasn't Looking' by Mary Rita Schilke Korzan. Copyright © Mary Rita Schilke Korzan. Reprinted with permission of Andrews McMeel Publishing. *Happy: A Children's Book of Mindfulness* by Nicola Edwards. Text copyright © Nicola Edwards, published by Caterpillar Books Ltd. Reprinted with permission of Caterpillar Books Ltd. *I Think, I Am!* by Louise Hay. Copyright © Louise Hay, 2008, published by Hay House Inc. *Can We Save the Tiger?* by Martin Jenkins and illustrated by Vicky White. Text © 2011 Martin Jenkins, illustrations copyright © 2011 Vicky White. Reproduced by permission of Walker Books Ltd., London SE11 5HJ, www.walker.co.uk. *Charlotte's Web* by E.B. White (Penguin Books, 2002), illustrated by Garth Williams. First published in Great Britain by Hamish Hamilton 1952, Puffin Books 1963. Copyright © J. White, 1952. Illustrations reproduced with permission of HarperCollins Publishers. 'Adventures of Isabel' by Ogden Nash. Copyright © 1931 Ogden Nash, renewed. Reprinted by permission of Curtis Brown Ltd. Extract from *Letters from Rifka* © 1992 by Karen Hesse. Reprinted by permission of Henry Holt for Young Readers. All Rights Reserved. *Around the World in 80 Days: Retold from the Jules Verne Original*, published by Sterling Publishing, 2007. Copyright © Sterling Publishing. *Tom and the Hippo-Pirates* by Hugh Madden. Copyright © Hugh Madden. Reprinted with permission of the author. 'Today is Very Boring' by Jack Prelutsky. Text copyright © 1984 by Jack Prelutsky. Used by permission of HarperCollins Publishers. Approx. 1,100 words from *Little Leaders: Visionary Women Around the World* by Vashti Harrison. Copyright © Vashti Harrison, 2018. 'Let No-One Steal Your Dreams' by Paul Cookson. Copyright © Paul Cookson. Used by permission of the author. 'Sky Rota: The Coolest 10-Year-Old Blogger We Know' by Casey Meehan, published on Independent Motors, www.independentmotors.ie. Copyright © Casey Meehan. 'Meet the 10-year-old blogger who cleans Dublin's beaches' by Paddy Woodworth, published in *The Irish Times*, 2017. © Paddy Woodworth. Reproduced with kind permission of author. 'My Family's Fond of Gadgets' by Kenn Nesbitt. Copyright © 2014 Kenn Nesbitt. All Rights Reserved. Reprinted by permission of the author. 'The World of Whales Explained' © *The Primary Planet Children's News Magazine*. 'Big Blue Whale' by Kathryn Apel. First published in NSW School Magazine, *Countdown*, 2008. Copyright © Kathryn Apel. Reproduced with permission of the author. Extract from *My Encyclopedia of Very Important Things* by DK. Copyright © Dorling Kindersley, 2016. 'I Built Myself a Time Machine' by Kenn Nesbitt. Copyright © 2014 Kenn Nesbitt. Extracts from *George's Marvellous Experiments* and *Revolting Recipes* by Roald Dahl. Copyright © The Road Dahl Story Company Limited. Reprinted with permission of David Higham Associates Ltd. 'Recipe for Disaster' by Kenn Nesbitt. Copyright © 2014 Kenn Nesbitt. 'I Am an Artist' by Pat Lowery Collins, illustrated by Robin Brickman. Text copyright © 1992 by Pat Lowery Collins. Reprinted with the permission of Millbrook Press, a division of Lerner Publishing Group, Inc. 'Science Homework' from *Revenge of the Lunch Ladies* by Kenn Nesbitt, copyright © 2007. Reprinted by permission of Running Press Kids, an imprint of Hachette Book Group Inc. *The One and Only Ivan* by Katherine Applegate. Text copyright © 2012 by Katherine Applegate. Used by permission of HarperCollins Publishers. *The Mysterious Neighbours at Number 33* by Sam Lawrance and illustrated by Andrei Verner. Text copyright © Sam Lawrance and illustration copyright © Andrei Verner. Reprinted with permission of the author. Extract and cover image from *Canary in the Coal Mine* by Madelyn Rosenberg. Text copyright © 2013 by Madelyn Rosenberg. Art copyright © 2013 by Chris Sheban. Used by permission of Holiday House Publishing, Inc.

The authors and publisher have made every effort to trace all copyright holders, but if any have been inadvertently overlooked we would be pleased to make the necessary arrangement at the first opportunity.

Contents

Writing to Socialise

Respect

Tom's Intro

Do you have a pen pal? Would you like one? What would you write to them about? What kinds of things would you tell them? What would you ask them?

We will start off our *Over the Moon* adventure by looking at the genre of **writing to socialise**. Letters are an example of this genre. Let's examine the format of a letter.

I have chosen to present an extract from *Dear David Walliams* by Tom Kelly. Wait a minute … that's me! I know what you're thinking: how do I have an extract in this book? Well, read on and you'll see – and maybe you'll get to know me a little better, too.

Before you start, I have a question for you: If you had to choose an author to write to, who would you pick and why?

Transfer of skills: People all over the world have been writing letters to each other for hundreds of years. I wonder what the word 'letter' is in other languages.

litir (Irish), *lettera* (Italian), *lettre* (French), *list* (Polish), *carta* (Spanish and Portuguese), *brief* (German)

Dear David Walliams

11 September

Dear David Walliams,

It's Tom here, Tom Kelly. You know, that famous kid from the *Over the Moon* series? Some people think I'm just a character in a book, but hey, <u>there's more to me than meets the eye</u>! It's tough being famous, isn't it? Everywhere you go, people <u>want a piece of you</u>.

Well, sometimes it's <u>not all it's cracked up to be</u>! Like when Mean Max from down the road called me 'Smelly Kelly' for no reason. It's like those kids in your book, *The World's Worst Children* – those beastly boys and gruesome girls can be <u>nasty pieces of work</u>.

Have you ever experienced something like this, David – you don't mind if I call you David, do you? So, what I'm asking is: how do you <u>cope with</u> the fame? And, how do you cope with the nasties?

Your overly famous friend,

Tom

17 September

Dear David Walliams,

It's been six days. Six days, three hours and forty-seven minutes <u>to be exact</u>. And. Not. A. Word. I know that you must get hundreds of fan mail letters a day, and I know that it is hard to reply to everyone, but I guess I was just hoping that you'd reply to me.

Anyway, you probably don't need to hear about what Max did the other day. <u>Believe it or not</u>, I now have a massive shiner. Boy, did it hurt. But I guess it will be gone in a few days, and who's going to notice anyway? My sisters Meg and Mel are in <u>a world of their own</u>, Mam works <u>round the clock</u> and Dad, well, Dad is living somewhere else now. I barely see him ... actually, let's just <u>park that there</u>.

Your running-out-of-patience friend,

Tom

Dear David Walliams,

Okay, I think I was a little too **harsh** in my previous letter. I know you're a busy guy – I read on Wikipedia that you are an actor, an author, a writer and a television personality. Woah, you're <u>living the dream</u>, man! But, can I just **clarify** something – isn't an author and a writer the same thing, and isn't an actor and a television personality the same, too? David, did you just get the folks at Wiki to make it look like you are actually greater than you are? Don't get me wrong, I have been known to <u>blow my own trumpet</u> every once in a while, but a word of warning, Dave: putting it up there on Wiki for the whole world to see is something you may want to **reconsider**! Like, what if your mother Kathleen or your sister Julie read it – what would they think? (And let's not even talk about the fact that your real name is Williams, not Walliams, and the only reason you changed it is because there was another guy called David Williams in your class and you didn't want the same name as him!)

But I'm **rambling**. What I meant to ask is this: Have you got any tips for how to avoid a lunch thief? Like, you know in *Gangsta Granny* how Ben and his granny were so **slick**: how can I be ready for the nasties when they attack? I really don't want any more 'ratburgers' in my lunchbox.

Cheers,

Tom (or you can call me Tombo – that's what my dad used to call me. I haven't seen him in four weeks now. He's not a 'bad dad' really, but Mam is <u>having none of it</u>.)

13 October

Dear David Walliams,

You've probably just replied to my other letter, but this one is on a totally different topic and I needed to get it off to you <u>ASAP</u>! Mr Hartnett has asked us to write to our favourite author with a list of questions. It's for authors' week. A bunch of them are writing to J.K. Rowling (another fake-namer) and Jacqueline Wilson (Meg and Mel have her entire collection). But obviously, I decided to write to you! You see, David, I feel as though you and I have a lot in common. I too have an 'awful auntie'. Her name is Emma and she stays on our sofa at the weekends. She insists that I bring her breakfast in the morning and **constantly** squeezes my cheeks and tells me I am <u>the greatest thing since sliced bread</u>. Like, seriously, does she realise I am not five anymore! I'm double-digits (well, nearly), and what's so great about sliced bread anyway? So Dave, here are my questions for you:

1. Is David Walliams your real name? (Come on now, tell the truth.)
2. Do you actually know a demon dentist?
3. Why do you write books for children?
4. Where do you get your ideas?
5. Do you have any kids?
6. What is your favourite book that you wrote?
7. Do you like to write books or do you just want to be rich and famous?
8. What is the title of your next book?
9. Which do you prefer more: being an author or being an actor … or a writer or a TV personality? LOL!
10. What is your favourite animal?

I need your answer by next Thursday. This is **urgent**!

<u>Yours sincerely</u>,

Tom

PS Please give me some tips on how to write a book.

PPS Mr Hartnett says I also need an autographed picture and a bookmark.

1 November

Dear David Walliams,

At first I was <u>pretty upset</u> when I didn't get an answer to my letter in time for authors' week, but I <u>worked it out</u> okay in the end. I read what it said about you on the back of *Grandpa's Great Escape* and I **blagged** the rest. I hope you don't mind.

When your letter *finally* came, I didn't want to read it to the class because I didn't think Mr Hartnett would like the silly answers (like that your real name is Joe King), but he said I had to. So I did and the class laughed, and I saw Mr Hartnett smirking.

I hid the second page of your letter from Mr Hartnett. That list of questions you sent for me to answer really made me mad. Nobody else's author put in a list of questions to be answered, and I don't think it's fair to make me do more work when I already wrote a report.

Anyway, thank you for answering my questions.

Yours truly,

Tom

PS When I asked you what the title of your next book was going to be, you said, 'Who knows?' Did you mean that was the title, or that you don't know what the title will be?

17 November

Dear David Walliams,

Mam found your letter and your list of questions, which I stupidly left <u>lying around</u>. She says I have to answer your questions because authors are working people like anyone else, and if you took time to answer my questions, I should answer yours. Maybe I'll get around to answering your questions, and maybe I won't. There isn't any law that says I have to. Maybe I won't even read any more of your books.

Disgusted reader,

Tom

2 December

Dear David Walliams,

I am sorry I was rude in my last letter. Maybe I was mad about other things, like Dad forgetting to send me a birthday card or Mean Max putting up a poster of *The Boy in the Dress* with a picture of me as the head.

Do you ever feel like you are <u>seen but not heard</u>, David? Like people can see you but not care what they say to you or what you have to say because they don't really see you. Do you get what I mean?

Still your No. 1 fan,

Tom

18 December

Dear David Walliams,

I bought a notebook like you said in your tips for how to become a writer. It is green with spiral **binding** and a picture of a gremlin on the back. On the front I stuck a label:

DIARY OF TOM KELLY

PRIVATE – KEEP OUT!

When I started to write in it, I didn't know how to begin. I felt as if I should write 'Dear Green Book', but that sounds silly. The first page still looks the way I feel. Blank. I don't want to be a **nuisance** to you, but I wish you could tell me what to do next. How do I write a diary?

Stumped reader,

Tom

TOM'S RESPONSE

So, as you can see, myself and David Walliams are <u>the best of buds</u>. I mean, sure, we <u>got off to a rocky start</u>, but he really is a great guy.

Hot seat   Imagine you are David Walliams. Reply to one of my letters.

Role-play   What should I say to Mean Max the next time I see him?

I found this picture of us Kellys all together. I wish we could go back to the way things were. I wonder when I will see Dad again.

Author's Intent

Why do you think the author wrote this piece? What message are they trying to get across?

When You Thought I Wasn't Looking

by Mary Rita Schilke Korzan

When you thought I wasn't looking,
You hung my first painting on the refrigerator
And I wanted to paint another.
When you thought I wasn't looking,
You fed a stray cat
And I thought it was good
to be kind to animals.
When you thought I wasn't looking,
You baked a birthday cake just for me
And I knew that little things were special things.
When you thought I wasn't looking,
You said a prayer
And I believed there was a God that I could always talk to.
When you thought I wasn't looking,
You kissed me good night
And I felt loved.
When you thought I wasn't looking,
I saw tears come from your eyes
And I learned that sometimes things hurt –
But that it's all right to cry.
When you thought I wasn't looking,
You smiled
And it made me want to look that pretty, too.
When you thought I wasn't looking,
You cared
And I wanted to be everything I could be.
When you thought I wasn't looking – I looked ...
And wanted to say thanks
For all those things you did
when you thought
I wasn't looking.

Writing to Socialise

Myself

Ella's Intro

Namaste (I bow to you)! Hello, my friends, and welcome to our unit on establishing a <u>growth mindset</u>.

This week we continue to look at the genre of **writing to socialise**. As well as writing letters, writing to socialise includes writing emails, blog posts, text messages and **affirmations**. Affirmations … what are those? Affirmations are words or statements that show praise and appreciation for what we are doing or trying to do in our lives. They are part of a growth mindset that helps positive thoughts flourish. We learn a lot about how to speak to and communicate with others. Today, we are going to think about how we speak to and communicate with ourselves.

I have chosen to present an introduction on what mindfulness is, followed by extracts from the books *Happy: A Children's Book of Mindfulness* by Nicola Edwards and *I Think, I Am!* by Louise Hay. Remember: Always respect how you speak to yourself.

Transfer of skills: Positive affirmations help us to have a growth mindset. Let's take a look at the word 'affirmation' in other languages. What do you notice?

dearbhú (Irish), *affirmation* (French), *afirmacja* (Polish), *afirmación* (Spanish)

Present in the Present

What is mindfulness? Mindfulness is noticing what is happening around you right now, what you see, smell and taste, how your body feels and what you mind is doing.

Mindfulness can help you to improve many areas of your life. When you start to notice what is happening around you, you **focus** more deeply. Improved focus can help you achieve at higher levels. Noticing what is happening around you can help you to calm down when you're feeling sad, angry or **frustrated**. Mindfulness can help you to <u>deal with</u> tough emotions. It can help you to feel better and focus on what is happening now rather than worrying about what has happened or what might happen.

Look at the different ways in which you can try out mindfulness.

Happy: A Children's Book of Mindfulness

Noticing

Real life is <u>right under our noses</u>,

We can miss it by rushing around,

But stopping to smell life's sweet roses

Is where true happiness can be found.

Relaxing

It's not just our minds we get trapped in,

Our bodies can feel **tension** too,

We can loosen our limbs when that happens,

Like the sun from the clouds, we break through.

*Try tensing up all of your **muscles** and then relaxing them, one by one.*

Loving

The warmth of a hug <u>can work wonders</u>,

Being happy is something you feed,

With a smile or <u>a touch or a kindness</u>,

Even the tallest tree grows from a seed.

Have you given someone a smile or a hug today?

Appreciating

It feels good to give thanks at the day's end

For the pink **blushing** sky overhead,

A hot meal, comfy shoes or a good friend,

And the warmth of a soft cosy bed.

What good things have happened in your world today?

Breathing

We breathe deep and expand like the galaxy,

We breathe out many thousands of stars,

And if ever we start to feel **panicky**,

This reminds us of just who we are.

Take a deep breath, hold it for two seconds and then breathe out very slowly.

Breathe in

Pretend you are smelling a flower.

Breathe out

Pretend you are blowing a leaf.

Appreciating

I Think, I Am!

Affirmations

Did you know that the things you think and say have the power to make a big difference in your life? When you say something <u>over and over</u>, you start to believe it is true. Learning to turn your unhappy (negative) thoughts into positive affirmations is a great thing to practise. Here's how it works.

NEGATIVE THOUGHT

Nobody likes me.

change to

POSITIVE AFFIRMATION

I love myself and other people love me, too!

I am present.

I am smart.

I am strong.

I am balanced.

I am powerful.

I am kind.

I am calm.

I am brave.

I am focused.

I am creative.

Tips for Doing Affirmations

1. Always start an affirmation with positive words such as 'I can', 'I am', 'I do', 'I have'.

2. Say your affirmation over and over, whenever you think of it.

3. Say an affirmation especially when you are having a lot of unhappy or negative thoughts.

4. Look in the mirror and say your positive affirmation out loud.

5. Write your affirmations down in a notebook or **journal**.

6. Make a sign with your positive affirmation and hang it where you can see it every day (like on your mirror or **bulletin** board).

Growth Mindset Statements

Read the following growth mindset statements to see how you can turn negative thoughts (a fixed mindset) into positive affirmations (a growth mindset).

Fixed Mindset   *Growth Mindset*

Instead of: *Try thinking:*

Instead of		Try thinking
I'm not good at this.	1.	What am I missing?
I'm awesome at this.	2.	I'm on the right track.
I give up.	3.	I'll use some of the strategies we've learned.
This is too hard.	4.	This may take some time and effort.
I can't make this any better.	5.	I can always improve so I'll keep trying.
I just can't do Maths.	6.	I'm going to train my brain in Maths.
I made a mistake.	7.	Mistakes help me to learn.
She's so smart. I will never be that smart.	8.	I'm going to figure out how she does it.
It's good enough.	9.	Is it really my best work?
Plan A didn't work.	10.	Good thing the alphabet has 25 more letters!

I am feeling energised and positive after reading that unit. How about you? Here are my affirmations. What are yours?

1. I will not compare myself to others.
2. I am an amazing person.
3. I am smart and capable of anything I put my mind to.
4. Today I choose to think the best of people.

Have you ever given yourself a compliment? It feels good. Give it a go!

AUTHOR'S INTENT

Why do you think the author of *Over the Moon* decided to include these extracts? Why do you think the authors of *Happy* and *I Think, I Am!* wrote these books?

Visiting Emotions
Anonymous

Where is the emotion visiting?
Is it inside your belly or close to your heart?
Is it heavy on your back or in your mind way up far?

How does the emotion look?
Is it small or is it big?
Short, medium or tall?
Does it shine or is it cloudy and dark?
What colours fill it, if it has colours at all?

How does the emotion feel?
Is it heavy or light?
Soft, hard or fuzzy?
Hot or is it cold?
Sharp, smooth or bumpy?
Is it a faint feeling or does it take hold?

How does the emotion sound?
Is it yelling loud or whispering?
Is it fierce, confident or shy?
Does it speak to you clearly?
Or does its voice quietly fade by?

What is the emotion saying?
Is it reminding you of something you know deep within?
Is it telling you something new?
What message is it delivering to brave and kind you?

Persuasive

The Environment

Evan's Intro

Good morning! How are you? Well, this morning I am feeling a little concerned. Have you ever thought about how animals become extinct? It is quite sad when you think about it. Is there anything we can do about it?

This week we are looking at **persuasive** texts. A persuasive text takes a point of view and makes an argument to support that point of view. A persuasive text tries to convince you that what is being said is correct.

I have chosen to present a **snippet** from *Can We Save the Tiger?* by Martin Jenkins. I have also prepared a piece for my home project on persuasive texts. I have used Martin's book as my **inspiration**.

Transfer of skills: Let's look at the word 'tiger' in other languages. What do you notice?

tíogar (Irish), *tigre* (Italian, French and Spanish), *tygrys* (Polish), *tigras* (Lithuanian), *tiger* (German)

Can We Save the Tiger?

Illustrated by Vicky White

The world's quite a big place, you know. But it's not that big, when you **consider** how much there is to squeeze into it.

After all, it's home not just to billions of people, but to the most amazing number of other kinds of living things too. And we're all **jostling** for space.

Us humans have changed the world a lot over the years, to make room for ourselves and to produce the things we need. We've turned forests into farmland, **dammed** rivers and built towns and cities to live in.

Some of the other animals and plants that we share the earth with have <u>coped with the changes</u> very well.

But some haven't.

In fact, some have coped so badly that they're not here any more.

They're **extinct**.

Which means we'll never see a live dodo …

Or a Steller's sea cow, or a marsupial wolf, or a great auk, or a broad-faced potoroo …

… or … I could go on and on.

A dodo   *A Stellar's sea cow*

See what I mean? This book <u>reels you in</u> and somehow shakes you into action. It makes me feel like I must do something to help the animals in danger of becoming extinct. But what?

I don't want to spoil the book for you, but I will ask you the same question that Martin Jenkins asks: Can we save the tigers?

My Home Project

There are so many animals <u>in danger of</u> becoming extinct.

I would like you to join me in taking a closer look at one of these <u>endangered species</u>. We are going to reflect on the **fearsome** but beautiful tiger.

As you may know, the tiger is the biggest species of the cat family. These fierce **felines** have walked the earth for a very long time. Fossil remains of tigers found in parts of China are believed to be two million years old! Yes, you heard me, two million years old. However, in the past 100 years, their population has decreased by 93 per cent. But why?

Today, there are six subspecies of tiger: Bengal, Siberian, South China, Sumatran, Indochinese and Malayan. Sadly, three other subspecies of tiger – Caspian, Bali and Javan – are now extinct. But why?

Bengal tiger

Siberian tiger

South China tiger

Sumatran tiger

Indochinese tiger

Malayan tiger

Many of these subspecies of tiger are endangered. Humans are the main cause of this through hunting and the destruction of **habitats**. But why?

Tigers can reach a length of up to 3.3 metres (11 feet) and weigh as much as 300 kilograms (660 pounds). An animal of this size needs a lot of space, of course. But so do people. So who deserves the space more: a tiger or a human?

If you have ever watched a documentary about tigers, you'll have seen that they usually hunt alone at night-time. Their stripes help them hide in the dense growth. When they're close enough – 30 to 35 feet away – they break from cover, race toward their prey and attack. Sounds **gruesome**, but tigers have to eat just as humans do, don't they?

In the same way that each and every one of us is special, so is the tiger. Every tiger in the world is **unique** – no two tigers have the same pattern of stripes. So why do humans feel that they have the right to kill these creatures?

A rare white tiger

It is sad to hear that there are more tigers held privately as pets than there are in the wild, don't you think?

Less than 100 years ago, tigers could be found throughout Asia. Sadly, hunting and habitat loss have put populations <u>at risk</u>, and today their **range** has been reduced to around 7 per cent of its former size. But why?

Tigers are becoming very rare because people hunt them for their skin and destroy the habitats they live in. The Bengal tiger has the largest population, with 3,500 left in the wild. The South China tiger has the smallest population, with only twenty or thirty left in the wild and about sixty in captivity. But why?

It is difficult to understand, but people continue to hunt tigers for their skins and kill them to use their bones and flesh in medicines.

What can we do to help?

1. Raise awareness.

2. Don't buy products made from tiger.

3. Adopt a tiger.

Can we save the tiger? It's up to us!

Evan's Response

I have been doing some research on animal rights. I found this website www.PETAkids.com. Here's their introductory statement.

PETA Kids is an animal rights organisation that helps kids aged twelve and under to learn about how to help animals! We believe that it's not cool to use animals for food, clothing, experiments or entertainment or to abuse them in any other way. Animals are our friends, and we are doing everything we can to make the world a better place for them. Find out how YOU can help animals, too!

How does this statement persuade you to join in and help save animals?

Wildlife conservation groups and tiger specialists are working hard to preserve and protect tiger habitats, but this costs money. I am going to do a fundraiser! Any thoughts on what I can do?

Did you know? Tigers are good swimmers and can swim up to six kilometres.

Did you know? Around half of tiger cubs don't live beyond two years of age. That's so sad.

Poll Who is the tiger's biggest enemy: other animals or humans?

Poll How long have tigers been living on this planet: two million years or 2,000 years?

Poll Which of these is not a type of tiger: Bengal, Sumatran or Catican?

Author's Intent

Why do you think the author wrote this piece? Why do you think Evan chose to do his home project on saving the tigers? Will you join him in the fight to save the tiger?

A Skip to Beat Bad Temper

by Cynthia Mitchell

An angry tiger in a cage
Will roar and roar with rage,
And gnash his teeth and lash his tail,
For that's how tigers rant and rail.
I keep my temper in a cage,
I hate it when it roars with rage,
I hate its teeth, I hate its tail,
So when it starts to rant and rail,
I tell my mum, I tell my dad,
I tell them why it's feeling bad,
And then I skip and skip and skip,
And lash my rope just like a whip.
And when I skip because I'm cross,
My temper-tiger knows who's boss,
And when I've skipped and whipped like mad,
My temper-tiger's not so bad.
I have to keep it tame this way,
Or it will eat me up one day.

Persuasive

Farming

Lainey's Intro

Dia dhaoibh, a chairde! Cad é an t-ainmhí is fearr libh? What is your favourite animal? Mine is a horse. I love their deep brown eyes and their shiny coats. I go horse riding *ag an deireadh seachtaine* with my brother and *mo chara* Jessica. It is so much fun. My horse's name is Millie. My brother loves the Labrador that lives with the stable owners. Abbie *is ainm di.*

This week we are continuing to explore **persuasive texts**. To persuade someone means to convince them that what you are saying is right. Have you ever persuaded someone to do something? You have to have a good argument and some clear points to prove why you are right. You also have to challenge the other point of view. Persuasive texts can be exciting!

I chose to present to you an extract from *Charlotte's Web* by E.B. White, illustrated by Garth Williams, as it shows how the character tries to persuade her father not to kill a pig.

Transfer of skills: I wonder what the word 'animal' looks like in other languages. Let's see. What do you notice?

ainmhí (Irish), *tier* (German), *animale* (Italian), *animal* (French and Spanish), *zwierzę* (Polish)

Charlotte's Web

Chapter 1: Before Breakfast

'Where's Papa going with that axe?' said Fern to her mother as they were setting the table for breakfast.

'Out to the hoghouse,' replied Mrs. Arable. 'Some pigs were born last night.'

'I don't see why he needs an axe,' continued Fern, who was only eight.

'Well,' said her mother, 'one of the pigs is a **runt**. It's very small and weak and it <u>will never amount to anything</u>. So your father has decided to <u>do away with it</u>.'

'Do away with it?' shrieked Fern. 'You mean kill it? Just because it's smaller than the others?'

Mrs. Arable put a **pitcher** of cream on the table.

'Don't yell, Fern!' she said. 'Your father is right. The pig would probably die anyway.'

Fern pushed a chair out of the way and ran outdoors. The grass was wet and <u>the earth smelt of springtime</u>. Fern's sneakers were **sopping** by the time she caught up with her father.

'Please don't kill it!' she sobbed. 'It's unfair.'

Mr. Arable stopped walking.

'Fern,' he said gently, 'you will have to <u>learn to control yourself</u>.'

'Control myself?' yelled Fern. 'This is <u>a matter of life and death</u>, and you talk about *controlling* myself.' Tears ran down her cheeks and she took hold of the axe and tried to pull it out of her father's hand.

'Fern,' said Mr. Arable, 'I know more about raising a litter of pigs than you do. A **weakling** makes troubles. Now run along!'

'But it's unfair,' cried Fern. 'The pig couldn't help being born small, could it? If I had been very small at birth, would you have killed me?'

Mr. Arable smiled. 'Certainly not,' he said, looking down at his daughter with love. 'But this is different. A little girl is one thing, a little runty pig is another.'

'I see no difference,' replied Fern, still hanging on to the axe. 'This is the most terrible case of **injustice** I ever heard of.'

A **queer** look came over John Arable's face. He seemed almost ready to cry himself.

'All right,' he said. 'You go back to the house and I will bring the runt when I come in. I'll let you raise it on a bottle, like a baby. Then you'll see what trouble a pig can be.'

When Mr. Arable returned to the house half an hour later, he carried a carton under his arm. Fern was upstairs changing her sneakers. The kitchen table was set for breakfast, and the room smelt of coffee, bacon, damp plaster, and wood smoke from the stove.

'Put it on her chair!' said Mrs. Arable. Mr. Arable set the carton down at Fern's place. Then he walked to the sink and washed his hands and dried them on the roller towel.

Fern came slowly down the stairs. Her eyes were red from crying. As she approached her chair, the carton wobbled, and there was a scratching noise. Fern looked at her father. Then she lifted the lid of the carton. There, inside, looking up at her, was the newborn pig. It was a white one. The morning light shone through its ears, turning them pink.

'He's yours,' said Mr. Arable. 'Saved from an **untimely** death. And may the good Lord forgive me for this foolishness.'

Fern couldn't take her eyes off the tiny pig. 'Oh,' she whispered. 'Oh, *look* at him! He's absolutely perfect.'

She closed the carton carefully. First she kissed her father, then she kissed her mother. Then she opened the lid again, lifted the pig out, and held it against her cheek. At this moment her brother Avery came into the room. Avery was ten. He was heavily armed – an air rifle in one hand, a wooden dagger in the other.

'What's that?' he demanded. 'What's Fern got?'

'She's got a guest for breakfast,' said Mrs. Arable. 'Wash your hands and face, Avery!'

'Let's see it!' said Avery, setting his gun down. 'You call that miserable thing a pig? That's a *fine* **specimen** of a pig – it's no bigger than a white rat.'

'Wash up and eat your breakfast, Avery!' said his mother. 'The school bus will be along in half an hour.'

'Can I have a pig too, Pop?' asked Avery.

'No, I only distribute pigs to early risers,' said Mr. Arable. 'Fern was up at daylight, trying to rid the world of injustice. As a result, she now has a pig. A small one, to be sure, but nevertheless a pig. It just shows what can happen if a person gets out of bed **promptly**. Let's eat!'

But Fern couldn't eat until her pig had had a drink of milk. Mrs. Arable found a baby's nursing bottle and a rubber nipple. She poured warm milk into the bottle, fitted the nipple over the top, and handed it to Fern. 'Give him his breakfast!' she said.

A minute later, Fern was seated on the floor in the corner of the kitchen with her infant between her knees, teaching it to suck from the bottle. The pig, although tiny, had a good appetite and <u>caught on quickly</u>.

29

The school bus honked from the road.

'Run!' commanded Mrs. Arable, taking the pig from Fern and slipping a doughnut into her hand. Avery grabbed his gun and another doughnut.

The children ran out to the road and climbed into the bus. Fern took no notice of the others in the bus. She just sat and stared out the window, thinking what a **blissful** world it was and how lucky she was to have entire charge of a pig. By the time the bus reached the school, Fern had named her pet, selecting the most beautiful name she could think of.

'Its name is Wilbur,' she whispered to herself.

She was still thinking about the pig when the teacher said: 'Fern, what is the capital of Pennsylvania?'

'Wilbur,' replied Fern, dreamily. The pupils giggled. Fern blushed.

Lainey's Response

Fern just saved that little pig's life! She stood up for what she believed in. I admire her for that.

I wonder why the book is called **Charlotte's Web**. I wonder what happens next.

I wonder if Fern will be able to take care of Wilbur.

What would you have done if you were in Fern's shoes?

What would you have called the pig?

Poll How many pigs do you think are there in the world: 250,000 or two billion?

Poll Where do you think half of the world's pigs live: Ireland or China?

Poll How many pigs do you think are killed each week: 23 million or 2,300?

AUTHOR'S INTENT

Why did the author write this story? Do you think the author likes animals? What message is he trying to send?

Adventures of Isabel

by Ogden Nash

Isabel met an enormous bear,
Isabel, Isabel, didn't care;
The bear was hungry, the bear was
    ravenous,
The bear's big mouth was cruel and
    cavernous.
The bear said, Isabel, glad to meet you,
How do, Isabel, now I'll eat you!
Isabel, Isabel, didn't worry.
Isabel didn't scream or scurry.
She washed her hands and she
    straightened her hair up,
Then Isabel quietly ate the bear up.

Once in a night as black as pitch
Isabel met a wicked old witch.
The witch's face was cross and wrinkled,
The witch's gums with teeth were sprinkled.
Ho, ho, Isabel! the old witch crowed,
I'll turn you into an ugly toad!
Isabel, Isabel, didn't worry,
Isabel didn't scream or scurry,
She showed no rage and she showed no
    rancour,
But she turned the witch into milk and
    drank her.

Isabel met a hideous giant,
Isabel continued self-reliant.
The giant was hairy, the giant was horrid,
He had one eye in the middle of his
    forehead.
Good morning, Isabel, the giant said,
I'll grind your bones to make my bread.
Isabel, Isabel, didn't worry,
Isabel didn't scream or scurry.
She nibbled the zwieback that she always
    fed off,
And when it was gone, she cut the giant's
    head off.

Isabel met a troublesome doctor,
He punched and he poked till he really
    shocked her.
The doctor's talk was of coughs and chills
And the doctor's satchel bulged with pills.
The doctor said unto Isabel,
Swallow this, it will make you well.
Isabel, Isabel, didn't worry,
Isabel didn't scream or scurry.
She took those pills from the pill
    concocter,
And Isabel calmly cured the doctor.

Recount

5

Emigration

Isabel and Carlos's Intro

Hola chicos y chicas (hello boys and girls)! *Qué pasa* (how are things)? We went to visit our *abuela* (grandmother) in Catalonia recently. It's always nice to travel back to where we come from; as the saying goes, there's no place like home!

This week we are looking at **recount** texts. When we write letters, we often recount events that have occurred. We let the reader know what has been happening and how we have been feeling. We tell them where we have been and who was with us. We can be personal or formal depending on the **recipient**.

We have chosen to present to you extracts from *Letters from Rifka* by Karen Hesse because it is based on a true story from the author's family. *Letters from Rifka* is about a family that have to leave their home. It presents a real-life heroine called Rifka who is full of courage and spirit.

Transfer of skills: Why is there no place like home? Here's what the word 'home' looks like in other languages.

baile (Irish), *maison* (French), *dom* (Polish), *casa* (Spanish and Portuguese), *hem* (Swedish)

Letters from Rifka

September 2, 1919

Russia

Poland

Russia

Ukraine

My Dear Cousin Tovah,

We made it! If it had not been for your father, though, I think my family would all be dead now: Mama, Papa, Nathan, Saul, and me. At the very best we would be in that filthy prison in Berdichev, not <u>rolling</u> <u>west</u> through Ukraine on a **freight** train bound for Poland.

September 3, 1919

Poland

Dear Tovah,

We were **fortunate** that we ran into no further trouble until we reached the Polish border. At the border, though, guards came aboard.

'Get off the train!' a squat man ordered. His round face and red cheeks did not match the <u>sharpness of his voice</u>. 'Get all your things and get off the train! Take off your clothes. A doctor must examine you before you enter Poland.'

October 5, 1919,

Motziv, Poland

Dear Tovah,

I thought we would be in America by now, but we remain in Poland, <u>stranded by</u> illness.

The sickness began with me. My legs and head started aching shortly after we crossed the Polish border.

I told Papa, 'I am tired. That spray has made me sick.'

By the time we arrived in Motziv <u>my head pounded</u> and my body hurt as if the train had run over me. I wanted only to rest. The **motion** of the train tormented me. I begged Papa for us to stop.

Mama and Papa took me off the train in Motziv. I did not know Papa had a cousin here, did you, Tovah? Papa's cousin did not have room for us, but he took us in anyway.

I don't remember very well what happened the first few weeks in Motziv. We slept on the floor in the shed of my father's cousin. I had dreams, terrible dreams about the guards at the train station and cossacks and entire forests chasing after me. Such nightmares!

I could not move at all. I felt imprisoned under a **mound** of stones.

I remember Papa down on the floor beside me, putting a damp cloth on my head. Papa is so good at nursing, but each time he placed the cloth over my eyes, I felt the weight of it crushing my head to the floor.

I tried to pull away from him, but whenever I moved, the pain exploded inside me. I begged Papa to stop, but the words would not come out. I could hardly draw breath, there was such a heaviness on my chest.

Saul says a student of medicine came to examine me. Papa had found a student to come who spoke Russian. By then a rash had crept under my armpits and across my back and my stomach. I had a cough that threatened to split me in two each time it erupted from me.

I had **typhus**.

The medical student said, 'Her infection started in Russia. Someone she had contact with there gave this to her.'

I wanted to tell this skinny, pock-faced man that he was wrong, that my illness did not come from Russia. I knew where it started. It came from the doctor at the Polish border. I tried to explain this to the man, but I could not speak.

'You must say nothing about <u>the nature of her illness</u> to anyone,' the medical student told Papa. 'Not even to your cousin. As for the child, she will probably die. Most do. That's how it goes with typhus.'

I remember very little, Tovah, but I do remember that. Those words <u>cut through</u> the fever and the pain. When I heard them, I wished I could die. If I died, I would be <u>free of my suffering</u>.

But if I died, I would never reach America.

I remember Mama crying. I tried to speak, to say I would not die, that nothing would hold me back from America, but she couldn't hear me. No one could hear me.

'I should send you all back to Russia,' the medical student said. 'But the child would never survive the trip.'

Papa begged him to let us stay. 'I promise to care for her,' he said.

The medical student agreed.

I **lapsed** into sleep on the floor in the miserable little shed while the typhus <u>raged inside me</u>.

Meanwhile, Mama and Papa and Nathan grew sick. They developed the typhus too. Only Saul managed to stay healthy. Saul is too much of an **ox** to get sick, Tovah.

Three men took Mama and Papa and Nathan in a cart to a hospital at the other end of Motziv.

I wept to see them go. I was still so sick, but I wept to see them. As they carried Papa out and loaded him into the cart beside Mama, I thought my life was over.

'Take me too!' I cried, but I had improved <u>compared to</u> Mama and Papa and Nathan.

'Motziv is full of typhus,' the car driver said. 'We need the beds for the dying.'

They left me with Saul, of all people. Saul who never has a kind word for me. Saul, who pulls my hair and punches me, even though Mama says at sixteen he <u>should know better</u>. Saul, with his big ears and his big feet, was all I had for a nurse.

It is a wonder I did not die from the typhus. When Saul remembered, he held water to my lips so I could drink.

In my dreams and when I woke, I <u>fretted over</u> Mama and Papa and Nathan. Were they already dead?

'Where is Mama?' I asked each time I woke from a **restless** fever sleep. 'Where is Papa?'

Saul turned his face away. He could not stand the smell of me; I could tell by <u>the way his mouth tightened</u>. 'Go back to sleep, Rifka,' he said. He always said the same. 'Go back to sleep.'

Once I woke to find Saul kneeling beside me, holding my hands down. His dark hair curled wildly around his ears. 'What are you doing to yourself?' he kept asking.

I had been dreaming about Mama's candlesticks. I was holding them against my chest. Hands, dozens of hands, reached out of the darkness to take them from me. I tore at the hands, trying to get them off me, trying to get them off Mama's candlesticks.

'Look what you've done to yourself,' Saul said, touching <u>the tail of his shirt</u> to my chest.

In my sleep, I had clawed at my chest until it bled.

Tovah, my hand is too weak to continue and <u>my eyes blur</u> at these tiny letters, but I will write again soon.

Shalom,
Rifka

November 30, 1919
Warsaw, Poland

Dear Tovah,

What should I do? I hold the worst news in my heart. Whatever shall I do?

October 22, 1920
Ellis Island

Dear Tovah,

This is the last letter I will ever write you from Ellis Island. It is almost impossible to believe what has happened today. I don't know where to start …

… I will write you tonight a real letter, a letter I can send. I will wrap up our precious book and send it to you too, so you will know of my journey. I hope you can read all the tiny words squeezed onto the worn pages. I hope they bring to you the comfort they have brought to me. I send you my love, Tovah. At last I send you my love from America.

Shalom, my dear cousin,
Rifka

Isabel and Carlos's Response

That sounds like a very **harrowing** journey. Poor Rifka and her family.

I wonder what happened on the rest of the journey to America.

If you and your family were forced to flee the country, what would you do? Where would you go? What would you bring with you? What would you miss most?

How scared must they have been when the guards came aboard the train?

I wonder why they had to flee their home in Poland.

Imagine what it was like sleeping on the floor in the shed and being extremely ill.

Poll Is typhus contagious? Yes or No?

Poll How far is Poland from the United States of America: 7,109 km or 71,090 km?

Poll 'Rifka' is the eastern European Jewish version of which name: Rebecca or Rosanna?

Author's Intent

At the end of *Letters from Rifka* there is an interview with the author. Remember we said that this book is based on a true story from the author's own family? What questions would you ask her?

From a Railway Carriage

by Robert Louis Stevenson

Faster than fairies, faster than witches,
Bridges and houses, hedges and ditches;
And charging along like troops in a battle,
All through the meadows the horses and cattle:
All of the sights of the hill and the plain
Fly as thick as driving rain;
And ever again, in the wink of an eye,
Painted stations whistle by.

Here is a child who clambers and scrambles,
All by himself and gathering brambles;
Here is a tramp who stands and gazes;
And there is the green for stringing the daisies!
Here is a cart run away in the road
Lumping along with man and load;
And here is a mill and there is a river:
Each a glimpse and gone for ever!

Recount

Travel

Tom's Intro

<u>I'm on top of the world</u> today! I am going on holidays with Mam and the twins. We are off to visit Auntie Emma who has gone to live in the Big Apple – New York! My bags are packed and it's time to <u>hit the road</u>. Statue of Liberty, here we come!

> This week we continue to look at **recount** texts. A recount retells an event in order. Recounts use time words such as 'First', 'Then', 'Next', 'After that' and 'Meanwhile'.

I have chosen an extract from *Around the World in 80 Days*, retold from the Jules Verne original. Can you imagine going around the entire world? Imagine all the different places you would see. Imagine the different types of weather, the food, the people … Imagine.

Transfer of skills: Do you know the word for 'world' in any other language? Here are a few. What do you notice?

domhan (Irish), *mondo* (Italian), *monde* (French), *mundo* (Spanish), *świat* (Polish), *welt* (German), *wereld* (Dutch)

Around the World in 80 Days

Extract from Chapter 1: Phileas Fogg Finds a New Butler

The entire day was planned. Phileas Fogg woke up at **precisely** eight o'clock in the morning. Breakfast was to be brought to him exactly twenty-three minutes later. At nine thirty-seven he liked to shave. Passepartout knew what he should be doing every second of every day. In fact, there was a system for everything! Even Mr. Fogg's clothes and shoes were numbered according to when they were worn, whether summer or fall.

Having seen the house from top to bottom, Passepartout said aloud, 'We'll get along just fine, Mr. Fogg and I. This is just what I wanted!'

Extract from Chapter 2: Phileas Fogg Says Something He Might Regret

Phileas Fogg left his house and walked the five hundred and seventy-five steps to the Reform Club. He went straight to the dining room and sat down at his usual table. Just outside the dining room was a garden that he liked to look at. Phileas's usual waiter brought him his usual lunch, which as usual, he finished at precisely twelve forty-seven.

After lunch, Phileas moved into the great hall to read the papers. He spent much of the day there and went back into the dining room for his supper. When he finished eating, he sat in the Reading Room with some other members of the club. At ten past six, he started playing cards with his friends.

Extract from Chapter 3: Phileas Fogg Shocks His New Butler

At twenty minutes before nine, Phileas and Passepartout found their seats in the **first-class** cabin. They made it to the train with five minutes to spare. Passepartout held on tightly to the carpetbag with **monsieur**'s money. He still couldn't quite believe what was happening. The train's whistle blew, and they were off!

Extract from Chapter 4: Introducing Detective Fix

The **whirlwind** trip had begun! In a mere four days of travelling, Passepartout and Phileas had already left Europe. They had travelled by train to Dover and then sailed to Paris from there. From Paris they took a train to Turin, Italy. Another train carried them through Italy to Brindisi, where they boarded a **steamer** called the *Mongolia*.

The *Mongolia* was due to arrive at the Suez Canal on Wednesday, October 9, at exactly eleven o'clock in the morning. It was one of the fastest steamers that Peninsular and Oriental Company owned. While the boat moved toward the Suez, two men walked up and down the canal …

Soon a few sharp whistles blew. The *Mongolia* was here! The **porters** rushed onto the dock and a number of boats rowed out to meet the steamer. The *Mongolia* dropped her anchor in Suez at exactly eleven o'clock – just as Stephenson had said it would.

Extract from Chapter 5: Phileas Fogg Travels Across the Red Sea and the Indian Ocean

The *Mongolia* left Suez on schedule — at exactly three p.m. local time — and started off on its journey to Aden. Phileas Fogg didn't care for **sight-seeing**, so he spent little time on deck. Instead he passed his time much as he did at the Reform Club — he ate his meals and played cards.

Unlike his boss, Passepartout truly enjoyed the scenery. He took every chance he could get to stand on deck and watch what passed by.

Fix tried to get Passepartout to tell him more about Phileas Fogg and his curious trip around the world. Passepartout always answered **honestly**, but he didn't know much. What little he could share was rarely of any interest to Detective Fix.

Meanwhile, the *Mongolia* pushed onward. They passed Mocha, drove through the Straight of Bab-el Mandeb, and then stopped at Aden for more coal. They were still sixteen hundred miles away from Bombay.

Fogg once again went on shore to have his passport stamped. He returned to the ship while Passepartout had a look around. By six o'clock, they were back on the ocean. The journey from Aden to Bombay was to take just seven short days. The Indian Ocean was smooth and calm. In fact, the *Mongolia* made excellent time. It arrived two days early!

When they reached the port, Phileas calmly entered the two-day **gain** in his diary. He also noted the time and the number of miles they had travelled.

After saying good-bye to his card partners on board the *Mongolia*, Phileas gave Passepartout some **errands** to run and set off in search of the passport office. They already had their tickets for the great railway that crossed India from Bombay to Calcutta. It was set to leave for Calcutta at exactly eight o'clock that evening. Phileas wanted Passepartout to make sure he was back by then.

With his stamped passport in hand, Phileas set off for the railway station to have his dinner. As for <u>the wonders of</u> Bombay, he didn't truly care to see them.

While Phileas tried to eat an awful meal of strange meat, Fix went off in search of the Bombay police station. He told them he was a detective from London <u>on the trail of</u> a robber.

TOM'S RESPONSE

Well, I <u>made it back</u> from New York <u>in one piece</u>! What a great adventure we had.

At precisely 07:06, we left for Cork airport. We drove there in Mam's grey Citroen Picasso. At exactly 08:16, we checked in and went through security. It wasn't long before we boarded the plane and set off on our trip. After ten hours and forty minutes in the air, we <u>touched down</u> at JFK International Airport. From there we hopped in a yellow taxi and navigated our way to Houston Street, where Auntie Emma lives. The first day we visited Ellis Island where we saw the Statue of Liberty. The second day we took a drive over Brooklyn Bridge. On the third day we all had fun in Central Park. On the last day we went to the Empire State Building to see the New York skyline. On the morning of 6 November, we took the long journey back home and <u>landed on our doorstep</u> at precisely eighteen minutes past five, just in time for dinner!

Author's Intent

How does the author use the five Ws (Who, What, Where, When, Why) in his writing?

Wynken, Blynken, and Nod

by Eugene Field

Wynken, Blynken, and Nod one night
Sailed off in a wooden shoe,—
Sailed on a river of crystal light
Into a sea of dew.
"Where are you going, and what
do you wish?"
The old moon asked the three.
"We have come to fish for the herring-fish
That live in this beautiful sea;
Nets of silver and gold have we,"
Said Wynken,
Blynken,
And Nod.

The old moon laughed and sang a song,
As they rocked in the wooden shoe;
And the wind that sped them all night long
Ruffled the waves of dew;
The little stars were the herring-fish
That lived in the beautiful sea.
"Now cast your nets wherever you wish,—
Never afraid are we!"
So cried the stars to the fishermen three,
Wynken,
Blynken,
And Nod.

All night long their nets they threw
To the stars in the twinkling foam,—
Then down from the skies came the
wooden shoe,
Bringing the fishermen home:
'Twas all so pretty a sail, it seemed
As if it could not be;
And some folk thought 'twas a dream
they'd dreamed
Of sailing that beautiful sea;
But I shall name you the fishermen three:
Wynken,
Blynken,
And Nod.

Wynken and Blynken are two little eyes,
And Nod is a little head,
And the wooden shoe that sailed the skies
Is a wee one's trundle-bed;
So shut your eyes while Mother sings
Of wonderful sights that be,
And you shall see the beautiful things
As you rock in the misty sea
Where the old shoe rocked the fishermen
three:—
Wynken,
Blynken,
And Nod.

Recount

Adventure

Meg and Mel's Intro

Hey guys! We're <u>on a mission</u>. A secret mission. We can't say much but it involves a bunch of ducks. They've stolen something precious belonging to our dear old granny. It's been in the family for years and we're going to get it back. Those pesky ducks will be <u>quaking in their boots </u>when they see what we've got planned.

This week we will look again at **recount** texts. As you know by now, a recount retells an event in order.

This week, we have chosen a short story by Hugh Madden. Hugh is an artist, **cartoonist** and street artist. He is from Cork but lives in Dublin. Hugh's piece is a **graphic** text. It is wordless. It is called *Tom and the Hippo-Pirates* and recounts an event where Tom and his hippo friend go into a tower where a group of **cloaked** birds dwell. Their aim is to **retrieve** a golden idol. But do they succeed? Dun, dun, duuun!

Transfer of skills: 'A picture is worth a thousand words.' Look at a graphic story or comic book from another country. Do you notice how the pictures tell the story? It doesn't matter what language you speak, the meaning is in the images.

Tom and the Hippo-Pirates

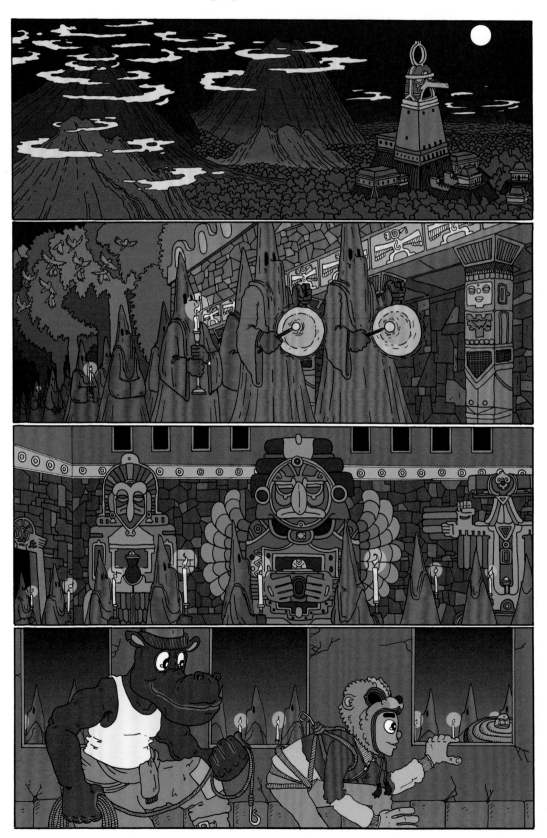

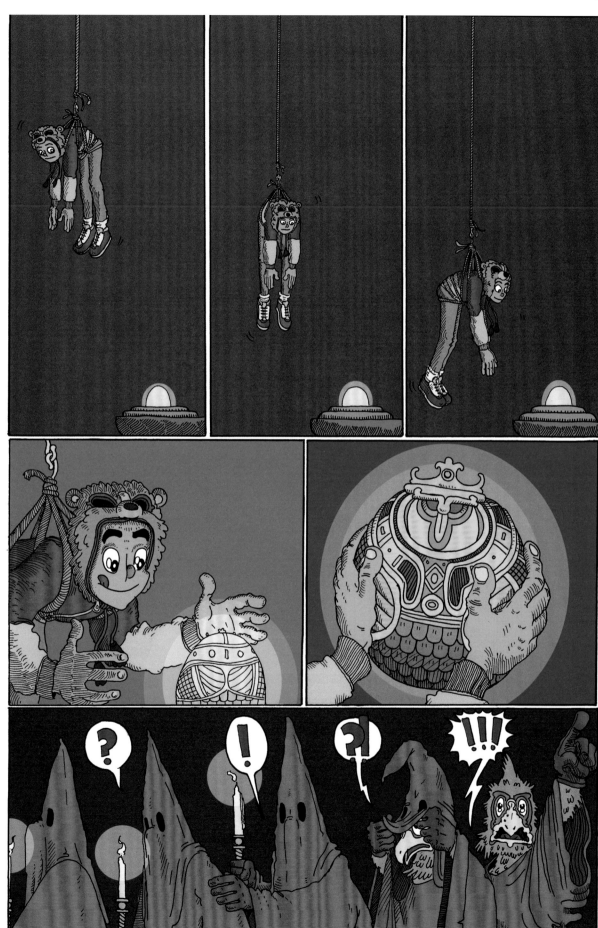

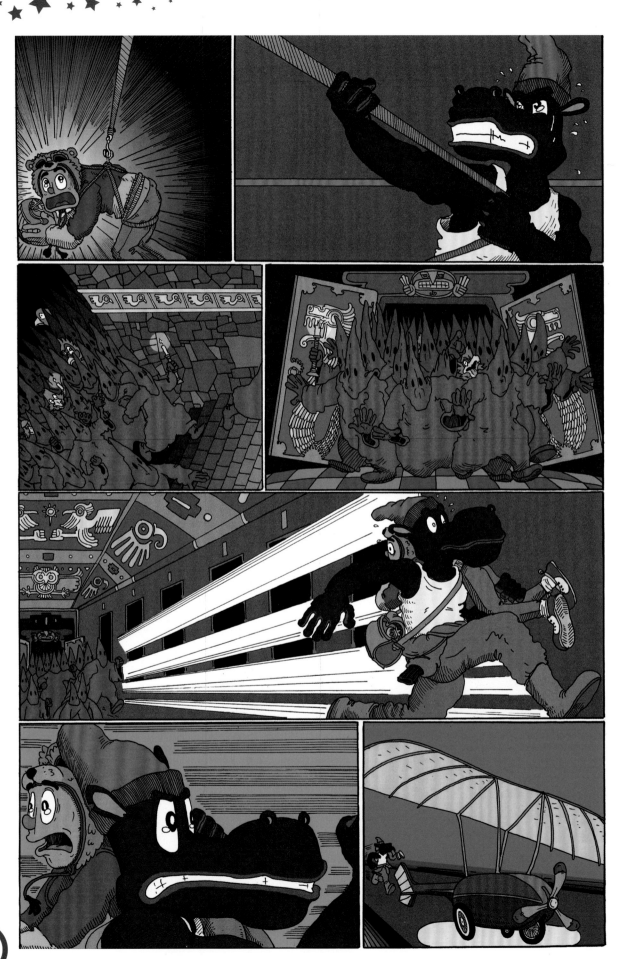

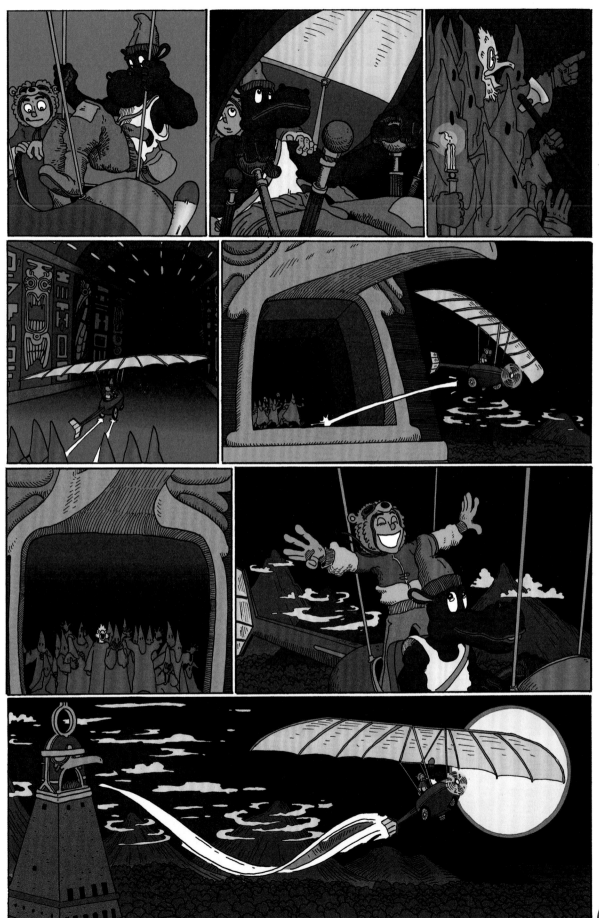

MEG AND MEL'S RESPONSE

I was on the <u>edge of my seat</u>, were you?

I didn't <u>move a muscle</u> waiting to see what would happen to Tom and Hippo.

So, here is <u>our take</u> on what happened …

Before they set off, Tom and Hippo planned their **mission** <u>to a T</u>.

First, they waited until <u>darkness had set in</u> before they made their way to the beaked tower.

Next, they watched as the cloaked birds marched <u>in single file</u>, with some of them holding **flaming** candles.

Then, Hippo got the rope ready as Tom **prepared** himself for what he was about to do.

After that, Hippo lowered Tom to the spot where the golden idol lay. With deep **concentration**, he clasped the idol in both hands.

Meanwhile, the cloaked birds continued to march.

Just then, one of the unhooded birds let out a scream, **alerting** the others to what was happening.

While this was going on, Hippo pulled the rope with all his might to <u>bring Tom to safety</u>. Tom was terrified but kept a **firm** hold of the **precious** object.

Next, the cloaked birds <u>rounded the corner</u> and raced up the stairs before bursting through the doors, inches away from Tom and Hippo. Tom had a look of <u>sheer terror</u> in his eyes, while Hippo ran as fast as his legs could carry them to their awaiting aircraft.

Eventually, despite the cloaked birds appearing not too far behind, Tom and Hippo managed to take flight into the night sky.

Finally, as the cloaked birds looked on in disbelief, Tom and Hippo **soared** to freedom, smiling at their **accomplishment**.

Why not put your creative hat on and try to make a graphic text of your own!

Author's Intent

Why do you think the author made this piece? How is being a graphic storyteller different to being a written storyteller?

Today is Very Boring

by Jack Prelutsky

Today is very boring,
it's a very boring day,
there is nothing much to look at,
there is nothing much to say,
there's a peacock on my sneakers,
there's a penguin on my head,
there's a dormouse on my doorstep,
I am going back to bed.

Today is very boring,
it is boring through and through,
there is absolutely nothing
that I think I want to do,
I see giants riding rhinos,
and an ogre with a sword,
there's a dragon blowing smoke rings,
I am positively bored.

Today is very boring,
I can hardly help but yawn,
there's a flying saucer landing
in the middle of my lawn,
a volcano just erupted
less than half a mile away,
and I think I felt an earthquake,
it's a very boring day.

Recount

Christmas

Ella and Isabel's Intro

Feliz Navidad, Feliz Navidad, Feliz Navidad, prospero año y felicidad. I wanna wish you a merry Christmas, I wanna wish you a merry Christmas, I wanna wish you a merry Christma, a **prosperous** year and happiness.

We are looking at the genre of **recount** once more. Recounts tell us the five Ws: Who, What, Where, When and Why.

We have chosen to present to you some Christmas legends, which recount the different traditions that come from all over the world. These give us an insight into why we do particular things when we celebrate Christmas.

Transfer of skills: I wonder what the word 'Christmas' looks like in other languages. What do you notice?

Nollaig (Irish), *Noël* (French), *Navidad* (Spanish), *Kerstmis* (Dutch), *Natale* (Italian), *Boże Narodzenie* (Polish), *Rozhdestvo* (Russian)

The Legend of the Poinsettia

There was once a brother and sister named Maria and Pablo. They were very poor, with barely enough to eat two full meals a day. As Christmas time approached, **festivities**, parades and parties in the village where they lived attracted all the local children. The **gaiety** of the season was quite **charismatic**. Moreover, a large manger scene was set up in the village church and the children were eager to visit the Baby Jesus and give him the best present. Maria and Pablo also wanted to give expensive presents to the Holy Child. While all the children were discussing what they would buy to give him, Maria and Pablo knew that they had no money to buy presents and had nothing that they could gift to the child.

Yet, they could not let go of the temptation to see the baby just once and give something to him. On Christmas Eve, Maria and Pablo <u>set out</u> for church a little earlier than the others to attend the service. Since they had nothing to give to the child, they thought of **plucking** some weeds that were growing along the

roadside to make a soft bed for Baby Jesus and to decorate his crib. While they were still decorating the crib, the other children arrived. Now, children can be very cruel when it comes to teasing and <u>making fun of</u> others. Maria and Pablo were almost in tears for shame and helplessness at their **mocking**, when a miracle occurred. Suddenly, the weeds burst into bright red petals that looked like stars and were so beautiful that everyone was **overawed** by their beauty. Everybody realised that a miracle had occurred and said that a gift of love is dearer to Jesus than the most expensive presents that money could buy.

Ever since then, poinsettia flowers have been a **favoured** Christmas decoration in many homes.

The Legend of the Baboushka

Christmas **heralds** a time **bonding** with friends and family and of spending time in the warm glow of love. Of course, gifts are an <u>eagerly awaited</u> part of Christmas.

The legend of the Baboushka is about an old and lonely woman who is considered to have started the tradition of giving gifts to children. Baboushka, which means 'grandmother' or 'old woman' in Russian, lived in a big house, safe and warm. However, she led a very lonely life with no company, friends or neighbours. Only the sound of travellers passing in their carts and the animals grazing nearby could break <u>the monotony of her existence</u>, these being her only **solace**. She would provide food to the animals and birds and offer <u>a resting place</u> to **weary** travellers.

When winter came – and winter in Russia is long and dreary – these little comforts would also <u>fade away</u>. Even the birds that she would leave crumbs for would desert her for warmer climates, leaving the old woman sad and lonely, wishing and praying for company. It was on one such winter's night, when she was trying to sleep, that she heard a noise <u>steadily</u> growing louder – voices and grunts – but she knew that there were no humans or animals for miles around, what with the entire earth being blanketed in snow. Before long, she heard a loud pounding at her door. She rushed to open it, thinking that it must be a cold and **famished** traveller, only to find three large horses with three noblemen dressed in what she thought was some of the finest and richest clothes that she had ever seen.

Baboushka invited the men inside, but they **declined**. Instead, they invited her to travel with them to Bethlehem, where they were bound, they said, to find and welcome the child who would be the king of Jews and lead mankind to **salvation**. Since it was night and the winter harsh, the old woman asked the strangers to **alight** and spend the night in her house so that they could all leave in the morning, but again they declined, saying that they did not want to delay. So they set off.

Later that night, she thought of the three men and the strange **tidings** they bore about the child who would be the king. She felt sad at **rebuffing** their invitation and so, then and there, she decided to set off in search of the child herself.

She gathered some **trinkets** to gift him and **ventured** out in the cold, dark night, but <u>try as she might</u>, she could not find the boy king. Legend has it that the old mother is looking for the boy king to this day and that whenever she meets a child, she presents him or her with trinkets and continues on her search. Thus from her comes the **custom** of giving gifts to children at Christmas.

The Legend of Christmas Stockings

In the story of Saint Nicholas – the patron saint of children – <u>lies the origin of</u> the tradition of hanging stockings up on the windowsill or near the **hearth**, in **readiness** to receive gifts from Santa. It is said to have started seventeen centuries ago in Turkey. Here the Bishop of Myra, Nicholas, was known all over for his **benevolence** and love of children.

One Christmas Eve, while he was passing a house, Nicholas heard a father and his daughters **lamenting** their poverty. The daughters could not be married because their father could not provide **dowry**, a custom that was **prevalent** in those days. Overcome with pity and sympathy, Nicholas noticed the woollen stockings that the girls had hung on the windowsill to dry, and he secretly placed enough gold pieces in each to provide dowry for them. Nicholas continued this tradition by distributing gifts secretly to children on Christmas Eve as a surprise for them.

In Holland, Dutch children put hay and carrots in their shoes for the horse of their dear Sinterklaas, a legendary figure based on St Nicholas who brings Dutch children gifts at Christmas time.

Swedish children wait for a kindly gnome called the Tomte instead of Santa Claus. This gnome is believed to live under the floorboards.

In some parts of France, Mexico and Spain, children wait for the Three Kings to fill their shoes with presents. Children of northern France, however, pray that Pere Fouettard, or Father Spanker, will not visit them as he is **reputed** to punish and spank children if they have been naughty!

La Befana visits Italian children and gives them gifts, **albeit** on the Epiphany (6 January). Agios Vasilis, the Saint of Letters, visits Greek children living on the plains, but those living in the mountains are taken care of by the tiny elves who bring the **desired** gifts to good little children.

Ella and Isabel's Response

Wow, that was interesting!

Who knew that there was a reason behind all of the things we do at Christmas?

My nana always buys a poinsettia at Christmas time and now I know why!

Have you ever seen a Baboushka doll? I have one. It has all the little baboushkas one inside the other.

Hanging out my stocking on Christmas Eve is definitely the most exciting time of the year for me.

Poll Bigger stocking = Better present: Yes or No?

Poll No chimney = No problem: Yes or No?

Poll White Christmas = Nice Christmas: Yes or No?

Why do people carry on traditions? What traditions do you have in your family?

If you were to create a new tradition, what would it be?

Author's Intent
Why did the author decide to include these pieces in this unit?

Christmas Long Ago

by Jo Geis

Frosty days and ice-still nights,
Fir trees trimmed with tiny lights,
Sound of sleigh bells in the snow,
That was Christmas long ago.
Tykes on sleds and shouts of glee,
Icy-window filigree,
Sugarplums and candle glow,
Part of Christmas long ago.
Footsteps stealthy on the stair,
Sweet-voiced carols in the air,
Stocking hanging in a row,
Tell of Christmas long ago.
Starry nights so still and blue,
Good friends calling out to you,
Life, it seems, will always slow ...
For dreams of Christmas long ago.

Report

Leaders

Isabel's Intro

Hola (hello)! *Que tal* (how are things)? *Tengo una pregunta* (I have a question): Who do you admire most? Why do you admire that person? There are a lot of people in the world who do amazing things. Can you think of someone, <u>past or present</u>, who has made a difference?

This week we are looking at **report** writing. We will look at reports on people. These reports tell us about their lives, the key points about them and what they have done. Dates and photographs or images are also used. It is important to keep reports factual.

I have chosen to present to you an extract from *Little Leaders: Visionary Women Around the World* by Vashti Harrison, as it is an interesting book all about women who have made a difference. They <u>come from all walks of life</u> and their talents are <u>across the board</u> – from **architect** to musician to navy **admiral** to **philanthropist**. Join me on our journey to get to know these wonderful women.

Transfer of skills: One of the pieces we are about to read is about a woman who was a musician and wrote songs. I wonder what the word 'song' looks like in other languages. Let's see.

amhrán (Irish), *sang* (Danish), *canzone* (Italian), *cântec* (Romanian), *chanson* (French), 歌曲 (*gēqǔ*) (Chinese)

Little Leaders: Visionary Women Around the World

Zaha Hadid

1950–2016

Architect

Iraq, UK

At eleven years old, Zaha knew she wanted to design buildings. Her mother let her <u>prove her skill</u> by decorating some rooms in the house. <u>It's safe to say</u> that, even as a child, Zaha had **impeccable** taste. Born in Baghdad, Iraq, Zaha studied maths at the American University in Beirut, in Lebanon, before heading to London to study architecture.

In architecture school, Zaha <u>followed the rules</u> her first few years, but for her final project she <u>let loose</u>. She was inspired by the work of the Russian **abstract** painter Kazimir Malevich and **re-envisioned** one of his works as a three-dimensional building. By graduation, she had made <u>a huge impact</u> at the school with her imaginative designs and **futuristic** ideas.

In 1979 she opened her own architecture firm in London. Zaha became known for her **dynamic** sculptural forms, often using curving shapes that swept through space and <u>flowed like water</u>. Her <u>bold approach</u> to architecture brought her attention and won competitions. Sometimes she was called the 'paper architect' because her designs rarely moved past the sketch phase. But soon the world caught on to Zaha's vision. Some of her **notable** buildings include the London Aquatics Centre, designed for the 2012 Olympics, and the MAXXI National Museum of 21st Century Arts in Rome; she also received the Pritzker Architecture Prize – and became the first woman to receive the field's <u>most prestigious award</u>. Her elegant buildings stand as her lasting **legacy** to the world.

The London Aquatics Centre

Violeta Parra

1917–1967

Musician

Chile

Violeta's musical career began at the age of nine. Her father, a music teacher, taught his large family how to sing and play guitar. Together, they toured Chile performing popular songs.

However, Violeta became interested in the country's traditional folk songs, which <u>were in danger of</u> being forgotten. In 1952, she **embarked** on <u>a life-changing journey</u> to rural villages, meeting with as many elders as she could find and **documenting** as many folk songs as she could hear. These songs had never been recorded or written down, and Violeta **logged** more than three thousand of them. She was **preserving** history and <u>making history</u> at the same time.

Violeta's own music changed in response. In particular, Violeta sang about human rights and <u>the gap between</u> the wealthy and the poor.

Violeta gained **recognition** throughout Chile and beyond. By 1954 she was performing across Europe, and eventually her recordings sold around the world. Her original songs were a hit, too. Her renowned single 'Gracias a la Vida' ('Thanks to Life') is still one of the most performed and recorded Latin American songs in the world.

Violeta was also a talented painter, embroiderer and **ceramicist**. She even exhibited her large embroidered tapestries at the Louvre Museum in Paris – becoming the first Latin American artist to have a solo exhibition there.

No matter what she was creating, Violeta's <u>singular goal</u> was to preserve Chilean culture. Today, as Violeta's songs are still being sung and recorded by a new generation of artists, she is celebrated as the mother of Latin American folk music.

Grace Hopper

1906–1992

Navy Admiral, Computer Scientist

United States of America

Grace always wanted to know how things worked. When she was seven, she **dismantled** her alarm clock just to figure out what was going on inside. Once she did, she easily put the clock back together! At college Grace studied maths and physics and later became a maths professor. She had a knack for explaining complicated **concepts**.

When the United States entered the Second World War, Grace wanted to help. The US Navy **rejected** her several times – once for being too small, and once for being too old. But Grace **persisted**, and in 1943 she joined the US Naval Reserve through the WAVES (Women Accepted for Volunteer Emergency Service) programme.

She was assigned to a special project: the navy hoped the Harvard Mark I, the first electromechanical computer in the United States, would provide **calculations** that could help with the war. But they needed someone to program it first. The computer (which was fifteen-and-a-half metres long!) was new to everyone but, as with her alarm clock, Grace figured it out. Her job was to write a book on how to use it – the first computer manual!

In 1949 Grace worked at a company overseeing the programming of the first **commercial** computer. Grace thought it would be easier if users could just communicate with it in English, but her co-workers <u>laughed at the idea</u>. Eventually she tried it, and her team ended up creating the **precursor** to COBOL, the most useful programming language ever.

When Grace was sixty, she returned to the navy to **standardise** computer languages. And when she retired at the age of seventy-nine, ending a <u>landmark career</u>, she was the oldest active-duty commissioned officer in the navy!

Perhaps Grace's greatest achievement was her translation of complicated ideas into simple language, something that <u>opened up</u> computing and **coding** for generations to come.

A publicity shot from 1952 of Grace advertising COBOL.

Fatima al-Fihri

Ninth century

Educational Philanthropist

Tunisia, Morocco

Not much is known about Fatima's life. She lived more than a thousand years ago! It was rare back then for a woman's story to be recorded, but Fatima left behind something pretty **remarkable**, so she will not be forgotten.

One of two daughters of a wealthy merchant, Fatima was both educated and **devout**. When she was a child, her family migrated from al-Qayrawan (in modern-day Tunisia) to Fes (in what is now Morocco). They were part of a large <u>influx of people</u> who brought a lot of business and culture to the city. But the majority of the new population was of Muslim faith – and there weren't enough **mosques** for everyone. Mosques are religious houses of worship that also serve as places for the community to gather.

When Fatima's father passed away, he left her and her sister a large **inheritance**. Both sisters wanted to use the money to help their community. Fatima decided to use her part to build the biggest mosque in North Africa. She **envisioned** it not only as a faith centre, but also a *madrassa* – a place of study.

Fatima was interested in architecture and **oversaw** the whole construction of the building. Named for the city of her birth, Al Quaraouiyine opened in 859. Over the next few decades the curriculum grew to include the natural sciences as well as religion, making it the first degree-granting institution in the world and a model for future universities!

In 1963, Al Quaraouiyine became an official state university in Morocco. In fact, it is the oldest operating university in the world. Long after she <u>passed away</u>, Fatima's vision lives on as scholars and the faithful continue to be educated there today.

Which visionary woman did you find most interesting? I really liked how Fatima al-Fihri used the money she inherited to do something good for others.

Aren't the shapes of Zaha Hadid's buildings really cool?

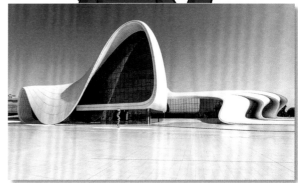

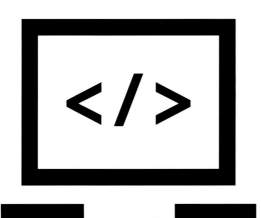

Have you ever tried to compose a song? You need a catchy tune and simple lyrics. My latest one is called 'A Little Sunshine' – you can check it out on GillExplore!

So we can thank Grace Hopper for paving the way for coding. Have you tried the Scratch programme? I'm still trying to <u>get the hang of it</u>!

Poll Who was born first: Zaha, Violeta, Grace or Fatima?

Poll Was Grace a musician or a navy admiral?

Poll Did Fatima live more than a hundred years ago or more than a thousand years ago?

AUTHOR'S INTENT

Why do you think the author collected all these stories and wrote this book? If you could choose someone to write about, who would you pick?

Let No-One Steal Your Dreams

by Paul Cookson

Let no-one steal your dreams
Let no-one tear apart
The burning of ambition
That fires the drive inside your heart

Let no-one steal your dreams
Let no-one tell you that you can't
Let no-one hold you back
Let no-one tell you that you won't

Set your sights and keep them fixed
Set your sights on high
Let no-one steal your dreams
Your only limit is the sky

Let no-one steal your dreams
Follow your heart
Follow your soul
For only when you follow them
Will you feel truly whole

Set your sights and keep them fixed
Set your sights on high
Let no-one steal your dreams
Your only limit is the sky

Lainey and Evan's Intro

Hey *Over the Moon* followers! We have started our own vlog. Do you know what a vlog is? The word 'vlog' is a combination of the words 'video' and 'blog'. A blog is a personal website or social media account that people upload posts or short articles to, so a vlog is a website where instead of posts or articles, we upload short videos! So we are now vloggers who love vlogging!

This week we are going to look at newspaper **reports**. Newspaper reports have some common features: a headline, date, name of reporter, captions, main text and images to accompany the text.

We tried to find the coolest reports for you. The following two reports, or articles, are about bloggers. Even though what they blog about is totally different, they both have something in common ... Look out for what it is.

Transfer of skills: There are bloggers and vloggers all over the world. Here's what the word 'blog' looks like in other languages. What do you notice?

blag (Irish), *blog* (French, German, Polish, Swedish, Spanish, Portuguese and Italian)

Sky Rota: The Coolest 10-Year-Old Blogger We Know

by Casey Meehan

1 June 2017

*Sky Rota, the ten-year-old blogger and car **enthusiast***

In the early fall, we wrote about luxury car **dealerships**, and that post caught the eye of another blogger. That blogger, who also happens to be in the fifth grade, reached out to us.

That's how we became acquainted with Sky Rota of Skycars.com.

Sky blogs about supercars, trips to dealerships to meet the people who sell these cars and **occasionally** what life is like for a ten-year-old.

Most of all, Sky has an **inspirational** story, but we'll let him tell that.

Last month we reached out to Sky to learn more about his world. Below is an interview with him, but first we wanted to give Sky the floor so he could introduce himself:

Sky: My name is Sky Rota. I am ten years old and in 5th grade. I live with my family and my pets in New Jersey.

I love to play basketball and baseball, I am an inventor and I design **prototypes** to make people's lives easier.

Most of all, I am an **exotic** car expert.

On the weekends, I visit car dealerships and check out the newest models of luxury cars and make friends with the dealers. The dealerships I have visited have been wonderful to me.

I even got to visit the famous Bugatti showroom in London. I write about all these experiences on my blog.

I started my blog in third grade, before I found out I was **dyslexic**.

My sisters built my blog for my birthday. They gave me a place where I could share my interest without getting <u>made fun of</u> for spelling words the 'wrong' way.

Since I was **diagnosed** with dyslexia last year, it has become more important to me to show people what it's like to go through school with a learning difficulty.

Even though I am not very good at reading and spelling, I have a lot of **strengths**. I am an athlete and an actor.

I love talking to people to learn and share new information, so recently I started my own YouTube channel vlog, SkyCars.

In my video visits, I take my viewers on fun, detailed tours of the **exteriors** and **interiors** of fast exotic cars like Lamborghinis, Rolls-Royces, Bugattis and Bentleys from a kid's <u>point of view</u>.

The Lamborghini Aventador S

Come on over to my blog and YouTube channel, and I'll show you how it's done, 'Sky-Style'!

See what we mean?! OK, here's our interview with Sky.

Independent Motors [IM]: How did you first get into exotic cars?

Sky Rota: The first car I fell in love with was my dad's Mercedes SL65 AMG. I used to play in it and make the convertible roof go up and down. My dad bought a special car seat for it so I could sit in the front seat. Now I am too big for the car seat but too small to sit in the front seat, so I am not allowed to go for rides in it anymore. That is how I started my journey of looking for exotic cars with back seats. I don't have a favourite car. There are so many amazing cars, I can't pick just one.

IM: Tell us about someone in your life you look up to.

Sky: Frank Kerbeck is my idol. F.C Kerbeck in New Jersey was the first dealership I visited. I wanted to take pictures and sit in his magnificent luxury exotic cars. I was on a mission, and Frank gave me the best day of my life. He let me sit in any car in his showroom. Then, he let my mom drive his Rolls-Royce Ghost while he and I sat in the back seat. It was the greatest experience ever.

The Rolls-Royce Ghost

IM: What have you learned about yourself since you began blogging?

Sky: Well, first I have to tell you that I have dyslexia. I am not the best reader or speller. When I blog, none of that matters. This is my own space, I don't have to worry about getting graded on it, and I can talk about all the things that interest me. I have learned that even though I have a learning difference at school, I can still **express** myself on my blog and my YouTube channel. I have many strengths, and I try to focus on the things I can do rather than things I can't do.

IM: What tips do you have for anyone else out there who might want to start a blog?

Sky: Go for it. If there is something that is interesting to you and you want to share it with the world, then a blog is a great place.

Sky Rota today – Sky has now written two books: one on his experience of having dyslexia and the other on 'the inside scoop on how Gen Z thinks, lives and operates'!

Meet the 10-Year-Old Blogger who Cleans Dublin's Beaches

by Paddy Woodworth

4 December 2017

When asked why he wanted to climb Everest, George Mallory replied: 'Because it's there'. Asked why she has taken on the challenge of clearing the rubbish from her local beaches, ten-year-old Flossie Donnelly takes a similar approach:

'I go crabbing in rock pools in Sandycove with my mum and we see rubbish and we pick it up. I go swimming and see rubbish in the sea, so I dive in and take it out.'

She first became aware of rubbish in the sea when **kayaking** in Thailand. 'It's a beautiful country, but there is an awful lot of plastic in the water. We filled a whole kayak with rubbish on our first day out. I hate to see the same thing building up in Ireland, so I want to help stop it.'

Flossie during one of her regular beach clean-up sessions

Her personal efforts have turned up a lot of garbage, ranging from a firework to a car battery to a full nappy ('yuk!'). She takes a **wry** pleasure in one particular discovery: a bridal bouquet, leading Flossie to invent lots of funny and dramatic scenarios about how it came to be in a rock pool, which you can read on her entertaining blog, www.flossieandthebeachcleaners.com.

This blog is just one of **several** tools that mark Flossie out as an organiser as well as an individual **activist**. She started with the help of her mother, Harriet Donnelly, and a few friends. They put up posters to ask neighbours to join them, but the results were **initially** disappointing.

'Posters just don't get awareness these days,' she says. She sought the help of the chair of the local council, Cormac Devlin, who advised her to use social media. Now there is a clean-up every week in summer, every month in winter, with the council supplying gloves and bags for the clean-ups.

Flossie has also managed to engage the help of a coastguard, Kryon O'Gorman, to get out on the water and clean Dun Laoghaire harbour, which she has found to be 'very dirty'.

Where does the rubbish come from? She is particularly **baffled** by cat food packaging, which she finds **repeatedly**, in large quantities, on a small beach she calls 'secret' because no one else seems to visit it. She wonders if it is being dumped by **commercial** shipping in storms, but cannot explain why it all ends up on the one beach.

Flossie is now fundraising for a sea bin for her area, a machine which **automatically** extracts rubbish from water pumped through it. 'Sea bins have never hurt a fish or a person,' she says. Of the €3,500 needed, she has already raised €1,017, 'and fifty cent'. Contributions can be made through her blog.

Flossie has also contacted a school in Thailand and has set up a 'virtual beach clean' in both countries for January.

What perhaps makes all these activities more remarkable is that Flossie is dyslexic. She recommends being **upfront** about this condition – 'that helps people understand when you make spelling mistakes' – and writing a blog as the best cure.

Her love of sea wildlife <u>shines through</u> her conversation, from starfish to octopus to dolphins. She greatly enjoys the growing local seal population, but wisely advises against swimming between a grey seal and her pups. 'Swimmers should understand,' she says, 'that we are intruders in their world.'

Her career ambition is to be a rock star, 'and write songs about cleaning the ocean'.

She says she finds the **current** state of the world environment 'very scary', but then reflects that <u>dire warnings</u> about the future were made in past centuries, too.

The future definitely seems just a little brighter to this environmentalist of a certain age after listening to Flossie Donnelly.

Flossie and some of the volunteers, helping to keep Dublin's beaches clean!

Lainey and Evan's Response

How cool are Sky Rota and Flossie Donnelly? Does this make you want to do something cool or start a new hobby?

I would love to ride in a fast car like a Ferrari or a Bugatti!

I think I'll try to organise a fundraiser for a sea bin for our local beach!

What scenarios do you think Flossie came up with for the bridal bouquet in the rock pool?

Did you figure out what Sky and Flossie have in common? Yes, they both have dyslexia. I wonder how that feels.

What are the pros and cons of having your own YouTube channel?

Flossie and I could be in the same rock band! What could we be called?

AUTHOR'S INTENT

Why do you think the authors wrote these articles? I wonder if the authors felt inspired by these ten-year-olds.

My Family's Fond of Gadgets

by Kenn Nesbitt

My family's fond of gadgets
and new technology.
My mother likes her radio.
My father likes TV.

My sister likes to dance around
the house with headphones on.
My brother plays on his PC
until the break of dawn.

The baby has a smartphone
and a touchscreen-tablet too.
If we had pets, I'm sure
that even they would have a few.

We chat with instant messaging.
We email and we text.
We're always looking forward
to the gadget we'll get next.

The power went out recently.
That day was like no other.
Our screens went blank and, strange but true,
we talked to one another.

Explanation

Mammals

Ella and Tom's Intro

Hey guys, how is the year going for you? What can you recall from our *Over the Moon* journey so far? We have another exciting adventure to bring you on, so best not <u>beat around the bush</u>. Let's get started!

> This week we are taking a look at **explanation** texts. Explanation texts explain how things/people/objects/animals work or do things. An explanation text presents and explains factual information. It tells you why or how something happens.

We have decided to present to you an extract from *The Primary Planet* news magazine. We love this magazine. Have you ever read it? When we saw the 'Cetacean Special' we knew you would have <u>a whale of a time</u> with it! The flash facts in this piece are a great example of the type of information you need in an explanation text. They seem to answer the questions that pop into your head as you are reading.

Transfer of skills: I wonder what the word 'whale' looks like in other languages. Let's see. What do you notice?

míol mór (Irish), *balena* (Italian), *ballena* (Spanish), *baleine* (French), *wal* (German)

The World of Whales Explained
CETACEAN SPECIAL

1. The word '**cetacean**' (pronounced *se-tay-shun*) comes from the ancient Greek language and means 'huge fish'. <u>It is no surprise</u>, therefore, that the members of the cetacean family include whales, dolphins and porpoises. Even though all members (over eighty in total) of this aquatic family live in the oceans and seas, they are mammals just like you and me.

FLASH FACT #1: A mammal is a warm-blooded **vertebrate** creature that feeds her young milk.

FLASH FACT #2: The word 'vertebrate' is used for mammals, birds, reptiles, amphibians and fishes with a backbone or spinal column.

(From left to right) Whales, dolphins and porpoises are all members of the cetacean family.

2. The blue whale is the largest member of the cetacean family, as well as the largest mammal in the world. It can measure up to 30 metres in length and can weigh close to 200 tonnes. Sadly, this magnificent creature has <u>suffered greatly</u> from over-fishing in the last two centuries and, as a result, is now listed as **endangered**.

3. The blue whale is part of the baleen whale group. They get their name from the baleen plates that hang from the roof of their mouths. These plates are made of a strong **flexible** material called **keratin** (a hard protein that can also be found in the hair, nails and skin of a human). They act like a

FLASH FACT #3: When an animal is classified as endangered, this means it is in danger of extinction.

The endangered blue whale

The baleen plates of a blue whale

sieve, allowing the whale to extract food (plankton, krill and small fish) from the water it pushes back out of its mouth.

4. Between the years 1908 and 1922, almost one thousand whales (including blue whales, fin whales and sperm whales) were killed by a Norwegian whaling station located in Black Sod Bay in Co. Mayo. Thankfully, in 1991, Ireland was declared a whale and dolphin **sanctuary** – the first of its kind in Europe. As a result, whale watching has become a very popular tourist activity, particularly off the coasts of Cork and Kerry.

5. The waters off the south-west coast of Ireland are a summer feeding ground for a large number of whale species including the fin whale, the **minke whale** and the humpback whale.

6. The humpback whale also belongs to the family of baleen whales and is one of the true giants of <u>the deep</u>. It can weigh in at over 35,000 kg and reaches lengths of 12 to 16 metres. It has a **bulky** head, two blowholes, a fluke tail (where the tail splits into two lobes, like that of the letter v) and two white flippers, generally about one third of its body length. The humpback's skin is frequently **scarred** and often covered with barnacles – a type of shellfish – that happily feed off the whale's dead skin.

FLASH FACT #4: The Irish Whale and Dolphin Group is dedicated to the **conservation** and better understanding of whales, dolphins and porpoises living in Irish waters. Part of their mission is to educate coastal communities on what they can do in the event of a live **stranding** (where a fish or mammal such as a dolphin or whale gets washed up on the beach, which can be a result of the creature getting caught up in the nets of large fishing trawlers).

Stranded whales on the west coast of Ireland

FLASH FACT #5: The fin whale has been nicknamed 'the greyhound of the sea', as it has <u>the build of</u> a racing yacht and could **outrace** the old steamships. The minke whale is the second smallest of the baleen category (the pygmy right whale is the smallest).

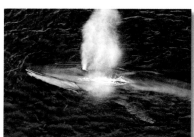

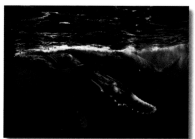

(From left to right) The fin whale, minke whale and humpback whale

7. The humpback whale gets its name from the way it arches its back out of the water <u>in preparation for</u> a dive. This dive is called **breaching** and scientists aren't sure if whales do it to get rid of pests or simply for fun.

8. The humpback whale is best known for its magical songs which can be heard over much of the world's oceans. Their songs are a <u>complex series</u> of sounds lasting ten to twenty minutes and can be repeated for hours at a time. These songs may have a role in mating.

9. A **narwhal** is a medium-sized whale that looks much like the **mythical** unicorn. The tusk-like structure that grows from its head is actually a tooth and can measure up to 3 metres in length. Females don't usually have this. Narwhals live in waters off Russia and Greenland, and in the Hudson Bay in Canada.

10. The largest of the toothed whales is the sperm whale. Sightings, however, are very rare, as they swim so deep in the oceans. They are also harder to locate than other whales, as they blow water through their blow holes <u>at an angle</u>, meaning the water they blow out isn't directly above their position in the water. They also have <u>the ability to</u> store oxygen in their blood, meaning they can stay under water for over an hour!

11. Because there is no light in the ocean depths, the sperm whale hunts using **echolocation**. This is where the whale produces a series of loud clicks. When the sound waves of these noises bounce back to the whale in the form of an echo, they can estimate the size and position of the prey ahead.

A humpback whale breaching

A narwhal

FLASH FACT #6: Narwhal mainly eat halibut, squid, shrimp and cod. They can dive to a depth of 800 m and remain underwater for up to 25 minutes!

FLASH FACT #7: The sperm whale gets its name from the spermaceti organ which fills most of its large head and produces a waxy substance called sperm oil. This was very much in demand in the eighteenth and nineteenth centuries as a fuel for lamps, in candle-making and in working with leather.

FLASH FACT #8: Although the sperm whale was depicted as a horrible monster in *Moby-Dick*, the famous 1851 novel by American writer Herman Melville, nothing could be further from the truth. In fact, even though the sperm whale has a mouthful of ferocious-looking teeth, it rarely uses them!

12. Dolphins are members of the toothed whale family and are very friendly, intelligent and playful creatures. They inhabit most of the oceans in the world, travelling around in large groups called pods. They are **generally** grey in colour. They are carnivores and consume a diet of fish, squid and crustaceans.

13. The bottlenose dolphin is the most common dolphin found in Irish waters. They are a large, grey, **robust** dolphin with a short stubby beak and a large dorsal fin. They are very vocal and can be heard producing a wide range of clicks and whistles. These sounds are used to navigate and find food, as well as to communicate with each other. Each dolphin has its own unique whistle.

14. The **Māui dolphin** is the rarest and smallest of all dolphins. It is only found off the west coast of New Zealand's North Island. It measures just over a metre in length and weighs about 20 kg. Compare this to the largest dolphin, the orca (commonly known as the killer whale), which can reach almost 8 metres in length and weigh over 860 kg.

15. From a distance, dolphins and porpoises can look alike. To tell them apart, first look at their heads. Here you will notice that the dolphin typically has a **bulbous** head and long beak. Porpoises, on the other hand, have a rounder face and a much smaller beak. The dorsal fins **differ** on both creatures too. The porpoise's dorsal fin is triangular, while the dolphin's dorsal fin is more curved. You may also notice that the porpoise is the shyer of the two around humans.

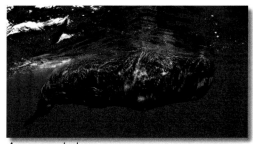
A sperm whale

A bottlenose dolphin and calf

FLASH FACT #9: A dorsal fin is the tall triangular fin on the back of a fish or whale.

FLASH FACT #10: In May 2014, the World Wildlife Fund (WWF) launched 'The Last 55' campaign as just 55 Māui dolphins were believed to be alive.

A Māui dolphin

16. Orcas, or killer whales, are the largest species of dolphin. They are called whales only because of their size. They have black skin with white patches and are found in all the oceans of the world. Individual orcas can be identified by their dorsal fin, which in males can reach 1.8 metres in length. They are the fastest sea mammal in the world, reaching speeds of 55 km per hour.

17. Often referred to as 'wolves of the sea', orcas live and hunt together in cooperative groups, also called pods. Groups of orcas herd fish into <u>compact areas</u> where they are easier to eat. They also slap their tails onto the water surface, **generating** a wave that can wash prey such as small penguins, seals or sea lions off the ice and into the water. They will also surround a larger mammal, such as a blue whale calf, and <u>wear it down</u> until it becomes exhausted, before moving in for the kill.

18. Like all mammals, cetaceans need their sleep. However, <u>sleep practices vary</u> between dolphins and whales. For example, dolphins sleep for similar periods to humans (up to eight hours per night), but only rest one half of their brain at a time! The other half stays awake to control their breathing. They then switch over to allow the working half time to rest. A sperm whale, <u>in contrast</u>, spends very little time sleeping. Fifteen- to twenty-minute naps are enough to rest this <u>gentle giant</u>. All cetaceans can sleep vertically or horizontally in the water.

An orca whale

FLASH FACT #11: Orcas get the name 'killer whale' because of their diet. They eat everything from fish to walruses, seals, sea lions, penguins, squid, sea turtles, sharks and, in some cases, other dolphins and whales. Their diet varies depending on the area of the ocean they are in, but an average-sized orca will eat over 225 kg of food a day! To achieve this goal, the orca must kill often.

FLASH FACT #12: Orcas are known as **apex** predators – this means that no other animals (apart from humans) hunt them. They are at the top – the apex – of the food chain.

FLASH FACT #13: Young whales and dolphins can fall asleep while swimming alongside their mothers. This is known as **echelon** swimming.

What do you call a baby whale?

A little squirt!

Ella and Tom's Response

Did you notice how the flash facts explained the questions that might have popped into your head as you were reading?

I wonder why some whales live longer than other whales.

I wonder what it would be like to sleep vertically.

I wonder what the humpback whale's magical song sounds like.

Quick Quiz

1. Where in Ireland can you go whale watching?

2. Name the most common dolphin found in Irish waters.

3. What is echelon swimming?

Author's Intent

What do you know now that you did not know before? How did the author of this piece keep us interested?

Big Blue Whale
by Kathryn Apel

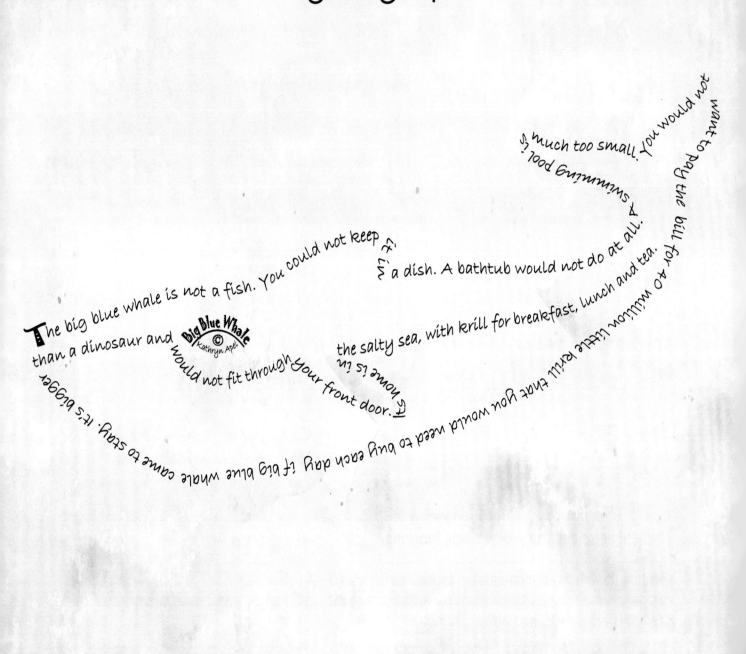

The big blue whale is not a fish. You could not keep it is a dish. A bathtub would not do at all. A swimming pool is much too small. You would not want to pay the bill for so many little krill that you would need to buy each day if big blue whale came to stay. It's bigger than a dinosaur and would not fit through your front door. Its home is in the salty sea, with krill for breakfast, lunch and tea.

Explanation

People

Carlos and Isabel's Intro

For Grandparents Day this year, we are preparing some interview questions. We are going to ask our grandparents questions all about their lives and how things have changed since they were young. Now that is <u>history in the making</u>! But what about life before that, and before that, and before that …?

This week we are studying **explanation** texts again. Explanation texts explain to us why or how something happens or happened.

We have chosen to bring you an extract from *My Encyclopedia of Very Important Things*. The extract is about how people lived long ago. It is interesting to see how people have changed and **evolved** over time. I wonder what children one hundred years from now will write about how we lived?

Transfer of skills: Do you know what the word 'history' looks like in other languages? Let's take a look. What do you notice?

stair (Irish), *storia* (Italian), *historia* (Polish), *histoire* (French), *geschiedenis* (Dutch), *geschichte* (German)

My Encyclopedia of Very Important Things

Very Early Humans

A lot of what we know about early people, we learned from things they made and their cave paintings.

Where Did They Live?

Early people would have to live near water, as lots of cave paintings show rivers and streams.

Cave Paintings

How Did They Make Cave Paintings?

Some drawings were scratched into rocks, but others were made with a kind of paint made from animal fat and **charcoal**.

What Do the Paintings Show?

Lots of cave paintings show pictures of people hunting for their food.

A cave painting showing a hunting scene

Early Discoveries

These **discoveries** seem so simple to us now, but they were all so important that it's impossible to imagine our world without them.

Fire

Learning how to make fire meant we could cook our food. Over time, this changed our brains and bodies, which **allowed** us to become clever enough to invent and discover other things.

How do fires start?

Fires start from increasing **tinder**'s temperature until it **combusts**. Tinder is a material that combusts first (as an ember or flame) and in doing so heats other material (heavier tinder, twigs, kindling, etc.) until it burns (as a flame).

The Wheel

We still use wheels to get around and move heavy objects, but before the wheel was invented we could only push heavy things or roll them over logs!

How do wheels work?

Wheels reduce **friction**. Instead of simply sliding over the ground, the wheels dig in and **rotate**, turning around **sturdy** rods called **axles**.

Tools

All sorts of jobs, such as hunting, making clothes and farming the land, became much easier when we started making and using tools.

How did they make the first tools?

Stone tools were made by taking a large piece of stone and knocking off smaller pieces or flakes, a process known as '**knapping**'.

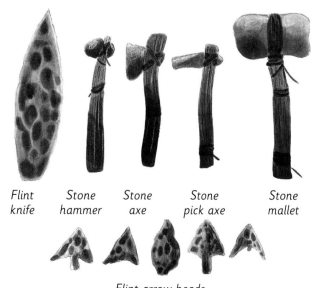

Flint knife   Stone hammer   Stone axe   Stone pick axe   Stone mallet

Flint arrow heads

The Time of the Pharaohs

A long, long time ago powerful people called **pharaohs** ruled over the land of ancient Egypt.

Mummy Mystery

When a pharaoh died he was made into a mummy and buried in a fancy box called a **sarcophagus** (pronounced *sar-coff-a-guss*).

How Were Mummies Made?

1. The body was washed and **purified**.

2. Organs were removed. Only the heart was left.

3. The body was filled with stuffing.

4. The body was dried by covering it with a substance called **natron**. This substance absorbed all the moisture from the body.

5. After 40–50 days, the stuffing was removed and replaced with linen or sawdust.

6. The body was wrapped in strands of linen and covered in a sheet called a **shroud**.

7. The body was then placed in the sarcophagus.

A sarcophagus

The Pyramids

The tallest building in the **ancient** world was the Great Pyramid of Giza. It still stands today.

The pyramids were built as tombs for pharaohs. Mummies were buried with special items such as jewels.

The Great Pyramid of Giza

How Were the Pyramids Built?

How the pyramids were built has been a mystery that **archaeologists** have been trying to solve for many years. It is believed that thousands of slaves broke down huge blocks of rock and then slowly moved them up the pyramid, piece by piece, on ramps. Scientists estimate it took at least 20,000 slaves over twenty-three years to build the Great Pyramid of Giza. Because it took so long to build them, pharaohs generally started the construction of their pyramids as soon as they became ruler.

Ancient China

During the country's long history, Chinese people have **manufactured**, built, discovered and invented many important things.

China's Four Great Inventions

Gunpowder, paper, printing and the compass are often called 'China's Four Great Inventions'. There aren't many things more important than paper. Without paper, you couldn't read this book!

Tea

Tea is very important to China's history. Many people still host special **ceremonies** with tea to this day.

What is Tea?

Tea is the second most consumed drink in the world, **surpassed** only by water. All teas (Black, Green, Oolong, White and Pu'erh) come from the same plant. The scientific name of this plant is *Camellia sinensis*. *Camellia sinensis* is a sub-tropical, evergreen plant native to Asia but is now grown around the world. 'Tea' is anything derived from the *Camellia sinensis* plant. Anything else, while sometimes called 'tea', is more accurately referred to as an herbal tea or **tisane**. Tisanes include chamomile, rooibos and fruit teas.

The Camellia sinensis *plant*

Silk

The Chinese figured out how to make silk from silkworm **cocoons** and used it to make kites and fancy clothes.

How Do Silkworms Make Silk?

Silkworms are the **offspring** of moths. They spew out thread from tiny holes in their jaws, which they use to spin into their egg-bearing cocoons.

Silkworm cocoons

Aboriginals

Who Were the Aboriginals?

The aboriginal people lived in Australia long before anyone else, and they still live there today. Their <u>way of life</u> has continued for thousands of years.

What Do They Believe In?

Spiritual People

Many Aboriginals feel <u>connected to the land</u>. They have many beliefs, stories and legends about how the world was created.

A Sacred Rock

Uluru is a massive rock that is very important to Aboriginals. At the bottom, there are caves filled with ancient paintings.

Many aboriginal people tell tales about the world through music, dance, stories and art.

What are Aboriginal Symbols?

Aboriginal art uses symbols to tell stories. This is what a few of the symbols mean.

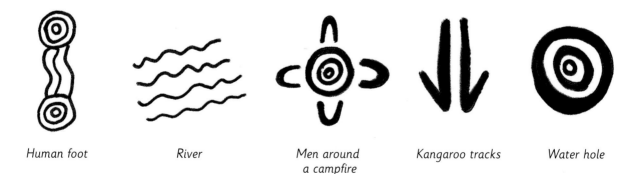

| Human foot | River | Men around a campfire | Kangaroo tracks | Water hole |

Carlos and Isabel's Response

If you had a time machine, what time would you like to travel back to?

I would like to see what life was like as an Egyptian pharaoh.

I'd like to go back a few thousand years and watch the Aboriginals do some cave art.

Check out the ancient Egyptian alphabet we found!

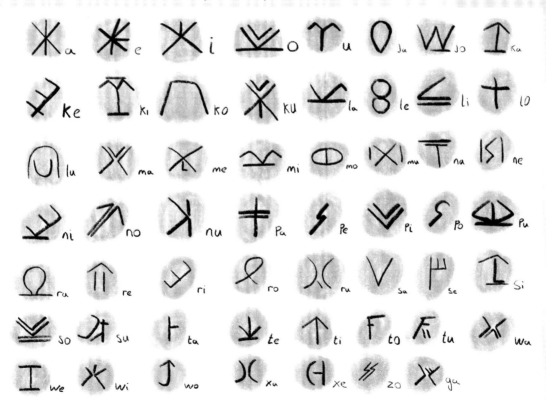

Can you draw the words 'pure' and 'kite' using this alphabet?

Can you make up some of your own words?

Author's Intent

Why do you think the author of *My Encyclopedia of Very Important Things* chose to write about these **civilisations**? What can we learn from people of the past?

I Built Myself a Time Machine

by Kenn Nesbitt

I built myself a time machine
tomorrow afternoon,
then travelled back to yesterday,
and very, very soon
I'll re-create my time machine
and travel once again
to yesterday where, like before,
I'll wait two days and then
I'll build myself a time machine.
I'm such a nincompoop.
I never should have made this thing.
I'm stuck inside a loop.

Procedure

(Food)

Ella's Intro

Welcome to Ella's kitchen! There is nothing I like better than cooking. I am learning that if you want to be a good chef you need to practise and experiment. You also need to follow recipes and plan out your dish.

This week we are looking at **procedures**. Procedures tell us the things we need to have and the steps we need to take to carry out something. A procedure could be in the form of a recipe, an experiment, a set of instructions to play a game or instructions on how to assemble something.

I have chosen to present a piece from Roald Dahl's *Revolting Recipes* because it combines two things: my favourite author (think *Matilda*, *The Twits*, *Charlie and the Chocolate Factory*) – and cooking!

Transfer of skills: Let's examine the word 'recipe' in other languages. What do you notice?

oideas (Irish), *recept* (Czech), *recette* (French), *rezept* (German), *recenta* (Spanish)

Revolting Recipes

Wormy Spaghetti

from *The Twits*

Serves 4 to 5

You Will Need:

● medium saucepan

● large saucepan

Ingredients (What Do I Need?):

2 tablespoons olive oil

1 onion, chopped

2 **stalks** celery, chopped (optional)

1 clove garlic, **crushed**

14 ounces canned plum tomatoes

1 tablespoon tomato paste

1 tablespoon chopped fresh parsley

1 bay leaf

1 teaspoon sugar

2 carrots, **grated**

salt and pepper

2 ounces fusilli

8 ounces **tricolour** spaghetti (2 ounces spinach, 2 ounces whole-wheat and 4 ounces regular spaghetti)

6 ounces Cheddar cheese

Method (What Do I Do?):

1. Heat 2 tablespoons of oil in a medium saucepan.

2. Cook the onion, celery and garlic over a low heat, covered, until soft.

3. Add the remaining ingredients for the sauce *except* the carrots. Bring to a boil and **simmer** for 30 minutes.

4. Remove the bay leaf and **purée** the sauce until **liquefied**. Return the sauce to the saucepan, season with salt and pepper to taste, and keep warm.

5. Meanwhile, bring a large saucepan of water to a boil and add a tablespoon of oil and a pinch of salt. Break the fusilli and the tricolour spaghetti into thirds and cook until **al dente**, about 5 to 10 minutes.

6. Fold the grated carrots into the sauce and heat through.

7. Serve the spaghetti on individual plates, topped with the sauce and grated cheese.

Snozzcumbers

from *The BFG*

Serves 8

You Will Need:

- vegetable peeler
- melon scoop (optional) or teaspoon
- paintbrush

Ingredients (What Do I Need?):

2 large cucumbers

1 can (3 ounces) tuna

1 to 2 tomatoes, **deseeded** and chopped

3 cocktail gherkins, finely chopped

3 tablespoons mayonnaise

2 teaspoons poppy seeds

salt and pepper

For the Coating:

a little extra mayonnaise

popcorn (cheese-flavoured popcorn tastes best)

extra poppy seeds

Method (What Do I Do?):

1. Peel the cucumbers.

2. With the pointed end of the vegetable peeler, cut several **grooves** down the length of each cucumber and carefully scoop out little holes at random between the grooves.

3. Cut off the ends of the cucumbers about 1½ inches from each end.

4. Hollow out the seeds from the body of the cucumbers using a melon scoop or a teaspoon.

5. Stand each cucumber in a tall glass and allow any **excess** liquid to drain (about 30 minutes).

6. Thoroughly drain the tuna and mix in the chopped tomatoes, gherkins, mayonnaise and poppy seeds. Season to taste with salt and pepper.

7. Using a teaspoon, fill the cucumbers with the tuna mixture, packing it down with the handle of the spoon.

8. Paint a little mayonnaise in the grooves on the outside of the cucumbers and carefully fill the grooves with poppy seeds. (A steady hand is useful!)

9. Place a small piece of popcorn in each hole between the grooves, putting a little mayonnaise in first to secure the popcorn. These can also be coated in poppy seeds if you wish.

10. Replace the cucumber ends.

Sophie said the original Snozzcumber tasted of frogskin and rotten fish. The BFG said it tasted like cockroaches and slime wanglers. What do you think?

Krokan Ice Cream

from *Boy*

Serves 4 to 6

You Will Need:

- **aluminium** foil
- baking sheet
- **skillet**
- rolling pin
- plastic bag

Ingredients (What Do I Need?):

2 tablespoons butter

3 ounces almonds, skinned and **coarsely** chopped

2 cups sugar

950 ml good-quality vanilla ice cream

Method (What Do I Do?):

1. Make the Krokan first. Lightly grease a piece of aluminium foil placed on a baking sheet.

2. Mix the butter, chopped almonds and sugar in a heavy skillet.

3. Place over a **moderate** heat and cook, stirring **constantly** and taking care that the mixture doesn't burn.

4. When it's a good golden colour, pour the mixture onto the greased aluminium foil.

5. Allow the Krokan to cool completely.

6. When it is cool, place it in a plastic bag and lightly crush it into small pieces by rolling over it with a rolling pin.

7. Let the ice cream soften at room temperature and then stir in the crushed Krokan until **thoroughly** mixed.

8. Place the ice cream mixture back in the freezer until it's frozen again.

'Krokan' is the Norwegian word for a delicious burned toffee mixture. The ice cream will keep for a couple of days before the Krokan begins to go soft.

Hair Toffee to Make Hair Grow on Bald Men (for moms to make only)

from *Charlie and the Chocolate Factory*

You Will Need:

- large heavy-bottomed saucepan
- small greased pan or tray
- sugar thermometer (optional)
- aluminium foil or plastic wrap

Ingredients (What Do I Need?):

4 tablespoons (½ stick) unsalted butter

1 cup plus 2 tablespoons sugar

1 tablespoon warm water

1 tablespoon white wine vinegar

2 tablespoons light corn syrup

4 ounces egg **vermicelli**, broken in half and cooked

Method (What Do I Do?):

1. Melt the butter in a large heavy-bottomed saucepan, stir in the sugar and remove the pan from the heat.

2. Add the water, vinegar and corn syrup, and stir over a low heat until the sugar **dissolves**. *Do not* allow the mixture to boil.

3. Add the egg vermicelli.

4. Place the sugar thermometer (if using) into the pan.

5. Now bring the mixture to a boil and boil **steadily** for about 15 or 20 minutes, or until the thermometer reads 152°C (305°F).

6. Pour the toffee into the greased pan and let it cool. As soon as it is cool enough to handle, lightly grease your hands with butter. Take two forks and scrape up some toffee with a few strands of vermicelli in it. Then, using your hands, roll the toffee into a small bite-sized mound. Repeat.

7. Place on a greased tray and allow to set.

8. Wrap and twist individually in plastic wrap or aluminium foil to prevent from becoming sticky.

ELLA'S RESPONSE

How excited are you on a scale of 1 to 10 to try out these recipes?! I'm a 10!

So, the original Snozzcumber tasted of frogskin and rotten fish, cockroaches and slime wanglers. Somehow I don't think this recipe will taste quite as bad!

Can you say 'spaghetti' and 'vermicelli' in an Italian accent? I'm working on mine!

What language does the phrase 'al dente' come from? What language does the word 'krokan' come from?

Poll Who thought there would be real worms in the wormy spaghetti?

Poll How many different flavours of popcorn do you know?

Poll Should I try the hair toffee on my dad who is bald? Yes or No?

AUTHOR'S INTENT

Why did the author write this piece? Can you think of a creative recipe? What would it look like? What would the ingredients be?

Recipe for Disaster

by Kenn Nesbitt

A box of melted crayons.
A cup of Elmer's glue.
A pint of watercolour paint.
Some Silly Putty too.

A half a pound of Play-Doh.
About a pint of paste.
A tablespoon of flubber
to improve the final taste.

I looked through all the cupboards
for things I could include.
If it was marked "Non-Toxic"
I just figured that meant "food."

To guarantee it's healthy
I topped it with a beet.
Then smashed it all together
so it should be good to eat.

I'm hoping that you'll try it
and tell me what you think.
Just close your eyes and open wide
and nevermind the stink.

Art

14

Ava and Lainey's Intro

Picasso said 'Every child is an artist'. So how do you become an artist? Let's start at the very beginning – a very good place to start. When you read you begin with a, b, c. When you count you begin with 1, 2, 3. When you draw you begin with … hmmm. Let's find out.

This week we are looking again at **procedural** texts. A procedure tells us how to do something. It shows us what to do step by step.

We have chosen to show you a piece that we have been working on with both the author and one of the illustrators of *Over the Moon*! As you may know, Ava and I attend art classes with Miss Evelyn at the Crawford Art Gallery. Recently we have been working on the **process** of drawing. When you break it down into steps, it is a whole lot easier. Don't believe us? See for yourselves!

Transfer of skills: Drawing is a **form** of art. Do you know the word for 'art' in any other language? Here are a few. What do you notice?

ealaín (Irish), *arte* (Italian, Spanish and Portuguese), *kunst* (Dutch), *sztuka* (Polish)

How to Draw

How do you draw? Well, there is a process to it. Just like any other process, there are steps to be taken.

How to Draw Faces and Expressions

Steps:

1. Examine the shapes of people's faces: some are round, some are long, some are square, some are oval. Draw the shape of face of your choice. We've chosen a round face.

2. Position the nose in the centre of the face. This can be a simple curved line to begin with. (You can practise drawing noses using the procedure on the next page.)

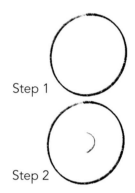

Step 1

Step 2

3. Next, take your ruler and measure the **distance** from one side of the face to the other. Now place two dots for eyes above the nose, at an **equal** distance apart. (You can also practise drawing eyes using the procedure on the next page.)

4. Directly above the eyes, position two eyebrows. Notice how the shape of the eyebrows can help show **expression**.

5. Directly across from the eyes, on either side of the face, draw two half love hearts. Now you have two ears!

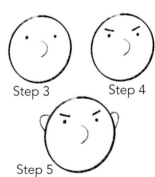

Step 3   Step 4

Step 5

6. Now observe the space that remains from the nose to the chin. Think of a facial expression: a smile, a **frown**, a shocked or sad face. Draw the curved line that matches the expression you are going for.

7. Decide on a hairstyle: long, short, curly, spikey … get creative! Ensure that both sides match for an even-looking style.

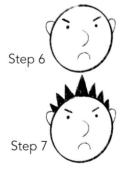

Step 6

Step 7

How to Draw Eyes, Nose and Mouth

<u>Let the pictures do the talking</u>! What is happening in each step below?

How would you explain what is happening?

Try to give instructions to your partner to create each of these facial features.

Ensure you have a good pencil and pay attention to the lines and **shading**.

Which facial feature was easiest/hardest to instruct/create? Why?

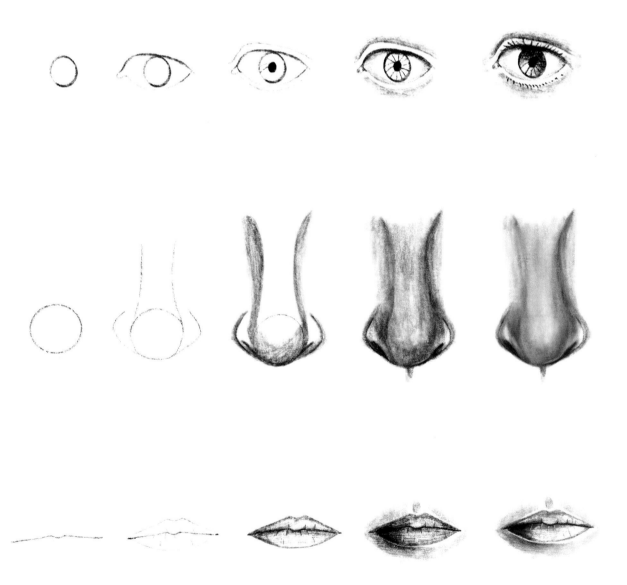

Explain to your partner how to draw a dinosaur and a pineapple! Use action verbs at the beginning of each step.

How to Draw a Dinosaur

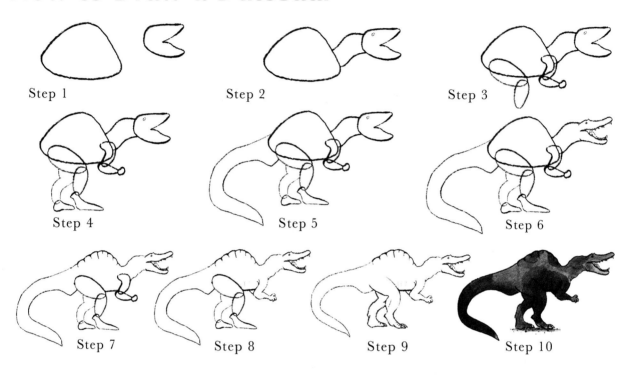

Step 1   Step 2   Step 3

Step 4   Step 5   Step 6

Step 7   Step 8   Step 9   Step 10

How to Draw a Pineapple

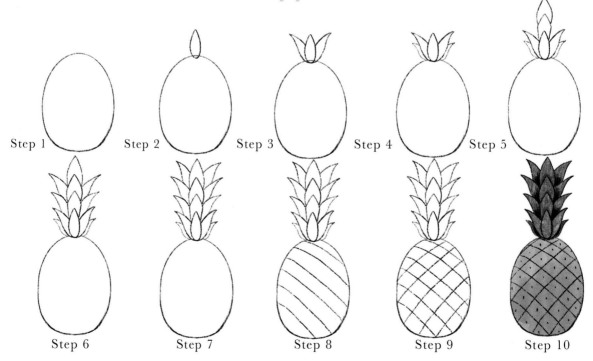

Step 1   Step 2   Step 3   Step 4   Step 5

Step 6   Step 7   Step 8   Step 9   Step 10

How the *Over the Moon* Characters Came to Life
By the illustrator, Charlie Alder

The first thing I had to do was to sit down and talk to the authors about the different characters and what they imagined them to be like. Often, when authors write, they have a **visual** image of the characters in their minds.

In *Over the Moon* – as you know! – there are two families: the Kellys and the Mooneys. We wanted to make each character different. We talked about the personality of each character and how to <u>bring that through</u> in their clothing and accessories.

For example, Tom likes wearing red and blue, so you'll often see him in that colour **combination**. Meg and Mel are twins but Meg wears glasses and Mel wears a hairband, so it's easier to tell them apart. (Notice too how the heights of the children show their age.) Tom's mum likes to wear a pendant that his dad got for her, and her favourite colour is purple so she will often wear purple clothes. You will notice how Luna the dog often has her tongue out to show how playful she is.

Ella is creative and likes to experiment with her style so we might see her in **patterned** leggings with shorts over them, a colourful top and a funky bun in her hair. Evan likes gadgets, so he is often seen with a phone in his hand. And baby Ed, well he likes to be cosy so he always looks cuddly in his outfits! Ella's dad wears a shirt, tie, trousers and smart shoes, so we can **infer** that he may work in an office. So as you can see, clothing can tell a lot about a person.

Here you see young and older versions of Lainey and Ava. Notice how they have changed and grown over time. When drawing full character sketches, I like to keep the lines and shapes simple. Notice how **classic** and clean-cut Lainey's outfit is. I am sure you have drawn T-shirts and trousers before. Do you see how I have added in little bumps at the waist and near the ankles to show where the clothes **crinkle**?

Body language is another feature to keep in mind when drawing. Look at how I have drawn Ava's hands behind her back in the first image. She has a slight smile on her face and upward-looking eyes, which **suggests** that she is looking up at someone but feeling a bit shy. In the next image, notice how her hands are **clasped** together in front of her. Now look at her circle mouth and downward-looking eyes. The illustration is supposed to make you think that Ava is worried about something. So, as you can see, a picture is worth a thousand words.

To **summarise**, here is my procedure for designing characters:

1. Meet with the author team and get to know the characters.

2. Make a list of personalities, likes and dislikes.

3. Decide on the age of each character.

4. Design a style for each character (clothing and hair).

5. Assign particular items to each character.

6. Depending on what is happening in the text piece, draw facial expressions and body language to match.

7. Get your creative hat on and add some colour and details!

Ava and Lainey's Response

We have been practising our drawing skills.

Ava has been working on roses and I have been working on my dog! What do you think?

Can you tell your partner the steps involved in the following drawings?

Ava's Rose – Step by Step

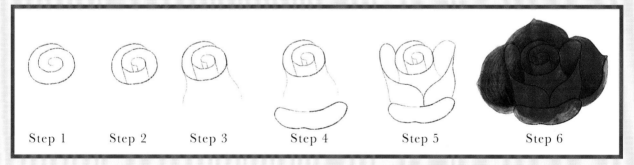

Step 1   Step 2   Step 3   Step 4   Step 5   Step 6

Lainey's Dog – Step by Step

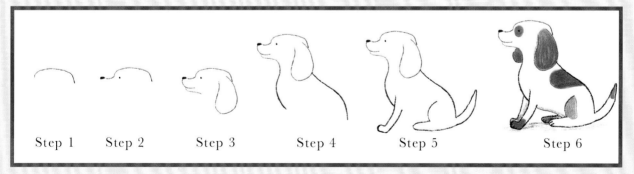

Step 1   Step 2   Step 3   Step 4   Step 5   Step 6

Author's Intent

Why do you think the author and illustrator of *Over the Moon* decided to include this piece? What questions would you like to ask the illustrator?

I Am an Artist

by Pat Lowery Collins

I am an artist when I follow a line where it leads me.

I am an artist when I find a face in a cloud

or watch the light change the shape of a hill.

I am an artist when I discover shadows made by the moon

or trace patterns in the sand

or when I name the colours inside a shell.

I am an artist when I look through a sun shower for a rainbow.

I am an artist when I find one.

I am an artist when I notice that the sea is a mirror for the sky

and when I make something from the things that I collect.

I am an artist when I shoot water loops in the air with the hose

or discover pictures in drops of rain.

I am an artist when I cut an apple to see the star inside

or when I watch sunlight turn dust to glitter.

I am an artist when I crunch through crusted snow

and stop to gather winter's hush around me.

I am an artist when I look at a bird until I feel feathery too

and at an orange until I know what it is to be perfectly round.

I am an artist when I run my fingers over a shiny pod or across the rough
   bark of a tree

or when I blow on a full-blown milkweed and it splinters into tiny white puffs

or when I pick up a maple-tree seed and send it spinning back to earth by its
   twin propellers.

I am an artist when I see that the sun comes up in a soft haze

and goes down in a fiery blaze.

I am an artist when I wait for a star to streak through the night sky

or when I sit very still in the woods and listen.

I am an artist whenever I look closely at the world around me.

And whenever *you* listen and search and see,

you are an artist too.

Procedure

15

Science

Carlos's Intro

Hola, que tal? What would you like to be when you grow up? I would love to be *un científico* (a scientist). I am always experimenting. I find the whole process fascinating.

> This week we will look at **procedural** texts once more. As we know by now, procedural texts tell us how to make or do something. They tell us what we need and the steps to be taken to carry out the procedure. You will see action verbs in procedural texts.

I chose an extract from Roald Dahl's *George's Marvellous Experiments* for you because I think you will really like it. After reading this you should be able to make your own putty farm, turn cola invisible, make flowers change colour and build your own speedboat. *Genial* (cool)!

Transfer of skills: Here's what the word 'experiment' looks like in other languages. What do you notice?

turgnamh (Irish), *expérience* (French), *experiment* (German), *sperimentare* (Italian), *eksperyment* (Polish), *experimentar* (Spanish and Portuguese)

George's Marvellous Experiments

Make Your Own Putty Farm

What You'll Need:

- a mixing bowl
- flour
- five eggs
- white craft glue
- water (cold is fine)
- your choice of food colouring

There are lots of methods for making squidgy silly putty that you can shape and mould, but most involve weird chemicals that are better used for unblocking drains or feeding to miserable old grandmas (but not your grandma!). This **version** is completely cleaning-product free and you can make your putty farm animals as GIANT or tiny as you want, just like George did.

What to Do:

1. Put two cups of flour in a big mixing bowl.

2. Crack in the eggs and mix them all together. Try not to think about cakes. Once the mixture is smooth, stir in three quarters of a cup of the glue, a little bit at a time.

3. Mix, mix, mix. Mix a bit more, slowly adding a few tablespoons of water until the mixture turns putty-like.

4. Add some drops of your chosen food colouring and mix it in. Use your hands to really squish the colour in there.

What's Happening Here?

With the flour, eggs and water, you're actually making a **basic** dough. The glue acts as <u>a binding agent</u>, which holds the mixture together, creating a **malleable** putty that can be stretched, shaped, squashed and bounced.

What If?

What happens if you use half as much glue?

What if you use twice as much?

Incredible Invisible Cola

What You'll Need:

● a small bottle of cola

● semi-skimmed milk

● a notebook or digital camera

Did you know that milk becomes a major ingredient if you add it to a bottle of cola? It turns the liquid as clear as water! George can get it from the cows on his farm, but you've probably got some in your fridge.

What to Do:

1. Unscrew the cap of your cola bottle and keep it safe. Carefully – and **preferably** over a sink – pour in enough semi-skimmed milk to fill the empty space at the top of the bottle. You want to fill it to the very **brim**.

2. Screw the top back on the cola bottle, being careful not to shake it up.

3. Keep the bottle on a level surface and check it every twenty to thirty minutes. Take a photograph or write notes each time, describing how it looks.

4. Eventually, all the milk will settle to the bottom in a lumpy brown **gunge**, leaving the rest of the liquid completely clear.

What's Happening Here?

The phosphoric acid molecules in the cola are attracted to the milk and attach themselves to the milk's molecules the first chance they get. The milk, laden with phosphoric acid molecules, **curdles** into lumps, which are much heavier than the other liquids in the drink. These sink to the bottom, pulling the phosphoric acid – and the brown colour – down with them. The lighter clear liquids that are left over then float on top.

What If?

How about trying a different kind of fizzy drink?

What happens if you shake the separated liquids up to mix them again?

Colour-Changing Carnations

What You'll Need:

- drinking glasses
- water
- white flowers (roses, carnations or even large garden daisies will all work)
- food colouring (a variety of colours)

White flowers are OK, but have you ever wished they could be more colourful? This experiment will show you how to go about colouring white flowers any way you like, and you certainly won't need brown shoe polish or dark-brown gloss paint like George to achieve it!

What to Do:

1. Pour water into your glasses and add a different colour of food colouring to each glass.

2. Cut your flowers so the stems are just a few centimetres longer than each glass. Place one or two flowers in each glass.

3. In an hour or two, you'll start to notice a change of colour, which will increase over the next few days.

What's Happening Here?

The colour of flowers is <u>partly determined by</u> the soil they are planted in and the water they drink. In this case, your flowers are drinking the coloured water (you may even be able to see it passing up the stem!) and the colouring is then being **absorbed** by the petals.

What If?

Ask a grown-up to help you carefully slit one stem in half lengthways and position the two half-stems (of the one flower) in two glasses filled with different coloured water. What happens?

What if you use a yellow or pink flower instead of a white one?

Build Your Own Speedboat

What You'll Need:

- a piece of thin card
- a clean plastic bowl or basin
- water
- washing-up liquid

Ever dreamed of owning your own speedboat? Well, now you can (sort of)! This experiment is quick and simple, and you'll possibly get wet ... so <u>let's dive in</u>.

What to Do:

1. Cut a boat shape out of your card, small enough so it has plenty of room in the bowl or basin. Carefully lay the shape down on top of the water so it lies flat.

2. Place a blob of washing-up liquid on your finger. Touch the water behind the boat, then watch it zoom across to the other side of the bowl.

What's Happening Here?

The boat stays afloat due to the <u>surface tension</u> of the water (water molecules sticking together to form a sort of 'skin' on top). By adding the washing-up liquid, the surface tension behind the boat is broken. The surface tension in front of the boat pulls it forward.

What If?

What happens if you try adding more washing-up liquid?

What other items can you make float?

Carlos's Response

> I think that Roald Dahl was one imaginative guy! What kind of person do you think he was?

Who knew flour, eggs and water could be used to make putty?

Is it just me, or is anyone else shocked that milk can turn cola clear?!

Let me get this right: if flowers drink coloured water and it is absorbed by the petals, they will change colour?!

Anyone know how to get food colouring out of my mum's favourite white T-shirt … Whoops!

Poll Which experiment would you like to conduct?

Author's Intent

I wonder if the author has conducted all of these experiments and did he have any difficulty with any of them.

Science Homework

by Kenn Nesbitt

I hope that you believe me
for I wouldn't tell a lie.
I cannot turn my science homework in
and this is why:

I messed up the assignment
that you gave us yesterday.
It burbled from its test tube
and went slithering away.

It wriggled off the table
and it landed with a splat,
convulsed across my bedroom floor
and terrorized the cat.

It shambled down the staircase
with a horrid glorping noise.
It wobbled to the family room
and gobbled all my toys.

It tumbled to the kitchen
and digested every plate.
That slimy blob enlarged
with every item that it ate.

It writhed around the living room
digesting lamps and chairs,
then snuck up on our napping dog
and caught him unawares.

I came to school upset today.
My head's in such a fog.
But this is my excuse:
You see, my homework ate my dog.

16

Narrative

Animals

Meg and Mel's Intro

We have a bit of a **predicament**. Can you help? Every time we go to our cousins' house, our two older cousins lock us in the toilet even though they know we don't like it. What should we do?

Have you ever been treated unfairly? How does it feel? What can you do if you are treated badly?

This week we are studying **narrative** texts. A narrative tells a story. A narrative text often has an introduction that grabs the reader's attention. The setting for the story is also described. Some characters are then introduced. We are given a hint of the problem to come. We can see all of these features in this unit's extract.

We chose the following text because we both love gorillas. We have a huge gorilla teddy in our room – it's just so big and cuddly! The text is called *The One and Only Ivan* and it's by Katherine Applegate.

Transfer of skills: I wonder what the word 'gorilla' looks like in other languages. Let's take a look. What do you notice?

goraille (Irish), *gorilla* (German, Italian and Latvian), *gorille* (French), *gorila* (Spanish and Portuguese), *goryl* (Polish)

The One and Only Ivan

Before you read this extract, examine the front cover, title and illustration, the name of the author and the Newbery Medal award stamp.

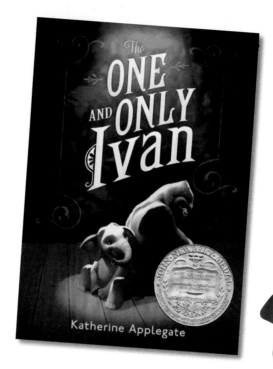

The Newbery Medal is awarded annually to the author who is **deemed** to have made the most distinguished contribution to American literature for children. It is named for John Newbery, an English publisher who lived in the 1700s. He was called 'The Father of Children's Literature' because of his **dedication** to publishing books for young people.

This is the book's blurb:

Ivan has lived in a cage in a shopping mall for most of his life. He rarely misses the jungle. In fact, he hardly ever thinks about it. Then he meets Ruby, a baby elephant, who opens his eyes and shows him that there may be another way to live …

Now let's read extracts from the book.

Names

People call me the Freeway Gorilla. The Ape at Exit 8. The One and Only Ivan, Mighty Silverback.

The names are mine, but they're not me. I am Ivan, just Ivan, only Ivan.

Humans waste words. They <u>toss them like banana peels</u> and leave them to rot.

Everyone knows the peels are the best part.

I suppose you think gorillas can't understand you. Of course, you also **probably** think we can't walk upright.

Try **knuckle walking** for an hour. You tell me: which way is more fun?

Patience

I've learned to understand human words over the years, but understanding human speech is not the same as understanding humans.

Humans speak too much. They <u>chatter like chimps</u>, crowding the world with their noise even when they have nothing to say.

It took me some time to recognise all those human sounds, to weave words into things. But I was **patient**.

Patient is a useful way to be when you're an ape.

Gorillas are <u>as patient as stones</u>. Humans, not so much.

How I Look

I used to be a wild gorilla, and I still look the part.

I have a gorilla's shy **gaze**, a gorilla's sly smile. I wear a snowy saddle of fur, the uniform of a silverback. When the sun warms my back, I **cast** a gorilla's majestic shadow.

In my size humans see a test of themselves. They hear fighting words on the wind, when all I'm thinking is how the late-day sun reminds me of a ripe nectarine.

I'm mightier than any human, four hundred pounds of pure power. My body looks made for battle. My arms, outstretched, **span** taller than the tallest human.

My family tree spreads wide as well. I am a great ape, and you are a great ape, and so are chimpanzees and orangutans and bonobos, all of us distant and **distrustful** cousins.

I know this is troubling.

I too find it hard to believe there is a connection across time and space, linking me to a race of **ill-mannered** clowns.

Chimps. There's no excuse for them.

The Exit 8 Big Top Mall and Video Arcade

I live in a human habitat called the Exit 8 Big Top Mall and Video Arcade. We are **conveniently** located off I-95, with shows at two, four and seven, 365 days a year.

Mack says that when he answers the **trilling** telephone.

Mack works here at the mall. He is the boss.

I work here too. I am the gorilla.

At the Big Top Mall, a creaky-music carousel spins all day, and monkeys and parrots live amid the merchants. In the middle of the mall is a ring with benches where humans can sit on their **rumps** while they eat soft pretzels. The floor is covered with sawdust made of dead trees.

My **domain** is at one end of the ring. I live here because I am too much gorilla and not enough human.

Stella's domain is next to mine. Stella is an elephant. She and Bob, who is a dog, are my dearest friends.

At present, I do not have any gorilla friends.

My domain is made of thick glass and rusty metal and rough cement. Stella's domain is made of metal bars. The sun bears' domain is wood; the parrots' is wire **mesh**.

Three of my walls are glass. One of them is cracked, and a small piece, about the size of my hand, is missing from its bottom corner. I made the hole with a baseball bat Mack gave me for my sixth birthday. After that he took the bat away, but he let me keep the baseball that came with it.

A jungle scene is painted on one of my domain walls. It has a waterfall without water and flowers without scent and trees without roots. I didn't paint it, but I enjoy the way the shapes flow across my wall, even if it isn't much of a jungle.

I am lucky my domain has three windowed walls. I can see the whole mall and a bit of the world beyond: the **frantic** pinball machines, the pink billows of cotton candy, the vast and treeless parking lot.

Beyond the lot is a freeway where cars **stampede** without end. A giant sign at its edge <u>beckons them</u> to stop and rest like **gazelles** at a watering hole.

The sign is faded, the colours bleeding, but I know what it says. Mack read its words one day: "COME TO THE EXIT 8 BIG TOP MALL AND VIDEO ARCADE, HOME OF THE ONE AND ONLY IVAN, MIGHTY SILVERBACK!"

Sadly, I cannot read, although I wish I could. Reading stories would make a fine way to fill my empty hours.

Once, however, I was able to enjoy a book left in my domain by one of my keepers.

It tasted like **termite**.

The freeway billboard has a drawing of Mack in his clown clothes and Stella on her hind legs and an angry animal with fierce eyes and unkempt hair.

That animal is supposed to be me, but the artist made a mistake. I am never angry.

<u>Anger is precious.</u> A silverback uses anger to maintain order and warn his troop of danger. When my father beat his chest, it was to say, *Beware, listen, I am in charge. I am angry to protect you because that is what I was born to do.*

Here in my domain, there is no one to protect.

Gone

Some animals live **privately**, unwatched, but that is not my life.

My life is flashing lights and pointing fingers and uninvited visitors. Inches away, humans flatten their little hands against the wall of glass that separates us.

The glass says <u>you are this and we are that</u>, that is how it will always be.

Humans leave their fingerprints behind, sticky with candy, **slick** with sweat. Each night a weary man comes to wipe them away.

Sometimes I press my nose against the glass. My noseprint, like your fingerprint, is the first and last and only one.

The man wipes the glass and then I am gone.

Shapes in Clouds

I think I've always been an artist.

Even as a baby, still clinging to my mother, I had <u>an artist's eye</u>. I saw shapes in the clouds, and **sculptures** in the tumbled stones at the bottom of a stream. I grabbed at colours – the crimson flower just out of reach, the **ebony** bird streaking past.

I don't remember much about my early life, but I do remember this: Whenever I got the chance, I would dip my fingers into cool mud and use my mother's back for a canvas.

She was a patient soul, my mother.

Poor Ivan. We just want to break in there and release him from that enclosure.

What do you think of the situation?

Ivan is tired of being locked up and stared at by humans. But what other choice does he have?

Flashing lights, pointing fingers, uninvited guests. I wonder how it feels to be stared at all of the time.

Ivan, Stella, Mack and Bob live at the Big Top Mall. How could their domains be made better? I am going to be an architect and re-design them!

Ivan has an artist's eye. He sees shapes in clouds and sculptures in stones. What shapes can you find in things around you?

Ivan has a memory of dipping his fingers into cool mud and using his mother's back as a canvas. I have a memory of having biscuits and juice at preschool and playing with Polly Pocket! What memories do you have?

Campaign I'm a gorilla – GET ME OUT OF HERE!

Can you make a connection between this text and any other we have read so far in *Over the Moon*?

Author's Intent

Why do you think the author wrote this book? What questions would you ask the author?

Being Brave at Night

by Edgar A. Guest

The other night 'bout two o'clock, or maybe it was three,
An elephant with shining tusks came chasing after me.
His trunk was wavin' in the air an' spoutin' jets of steam
An' he was out to eat me up, but still I didn't scream
Or let him see that I was scared – a better thought I had,
I just escaped from where I was and crawled in bed with Dad.

One time there was a giant who was horrible to see,
He had three heads and twenty arms, an' he came after me
And red hot fire came from his mouths and every hand was red
And he declared he'd grind my bones and make them into bread.
But I was just too smart for him, I fooled him mighty bad,
Before his hands could collar me I crawled in bed with Dad.

I ain't scared of nothin' that comes pesterin' me at night.
Once I was chased by forty ghosts all shimmery an' white.
An' I just raced 'em round the room an' let 'em think maybe
I'd have to stop an' rest awhile, when they could capture me.
Then when they leapt onto my bed, Oh Gee! But they were mad
To find that I had slipped away an' crawled in bed with Dad.

No giants, ghosts or elephants have dared to come in there
'Coz if they did he'd beat 'em up and chase 'em to their lair.
They just hang 'round the children's rooms
an' snap an' snarl an' bite
An' laugh if they can make 'em yell
for help with all their might.
But I don't ever yell out loud. I'm not that sort of lad,
I slip from out the covers and I crawl in bed with Dad.

Narrative

At Home

Ella's Intro

Hey guys, how's tricks? Do you have a next-door neighbour? What are they like? In our extract today there are some pretty spooky new neighbours! So, if there's something strange in the neighbourhood, who you gonna call?

This week we're studying **narrative** texts again. A narrative is a spoken or written account of connected events. A narrative will usually have a setting (place), characters (people/creatures), dialogue (talking), atmosphere (mood) and a problem that needs to be solved. Narrative texts like to <u>hook</u> the reader and <u>reel them in</u>. This can be done through dialogue, questions, vivid description, interesting facts or sound effects. Examples of hooks include 'Have you ever …' or 'Did you know …'

The extract that I have chosen for you is called *The Mysterious Neighbours at Number 33* by Sam Lawrance. Sam is a primary school teacher from Cork. I chose this text because I have a feeling that a neighbour of mine may very well be a vampire! I need to do some <u>detective work</u>. Let's read on …

Transfer of skills: Neighbours are people who live near us. Let's look at the word 'neighbour' in other languages. What do you notice?

comharsa (Irish), *nachbar* (German), *vicino* (Italian), *sąsiad* (Polish), 鄰居 (línjū) (Chinese)

The Mysterious Neighbours at Number 33

Illustrated by Andrei Verner

Vampires

The story you are about to read is about vampires. And it is a true story!

I know what you're thinking. You think vampires are the stuff of fairy tales. That they're make believe – like fairies, unicorns, dragons, or teachers with a sense of humour. But you are wrong. Dead wrong! Vampires are real! And while most of you reading this will probably never **encounter** one, they are out there, hiding in the shadows of villages, towns and cities across the world.

So, before I begin this story, I feel I must give you some information on vampires. You need to know their habits and what makes them tick. And most importantly, you need to know how you can protect yourself, should you ever come across one! I couldn't bear it if you were only two chapters into this book and discovered that a vampire was living nearby and you didn't know what to do. So, I beg you, please read the following chapters very carefully. This information could one day save your life!

I will begin with a fact that you probably already know – that vampires drink blood. But what you can't imagine is how much they **crave** it. Vampires have a thirst for blood that is unimaginable to you or I. Cast your mind back to the time when you were the thirstiest you've ever been. I should imagine it was during a long hot summer's day after you had been foolishly running around with your friends. You were probably dripping in sweat and had a face the colour of an embarrassed strawberry. Do you remember how your throat felt like the skin of a cactus being scraped by rough sandpaper? And do you recall how good that drink felt as it slipped down your throat? It may have been an ice cold can of your favourite fizzy pop, it could have been a freshly squeezed orange juice in a tall tumbler, or it might have been a glass of ordinary tap water, but whatever it was, that feeling you had when you **guzzled** that drink was one of complete joy. A vampire feels this thirst all of the time, and they only get the **sensation** of total refreshment when that rich cherry blood passes their pale lips. So you can understand why they want it so badly!

Now, I tell you this as I want you to realise something — if you come across a vampire, they will want to drain you of every drop of your precious blood. You will not be able to reason with the creature, plead with it, or beg for mercy. There are but two choices — you run for your life, or you kill the vampire. Failing in this will lead to only one outcome ... your **untimely** death!

By this point, you may have noticed that when I talk of vampires I use the word *it*, and not he or she. That's because vampires aren't human. Despite looking human in many ways, vampires are actually a totally different species altogether. Vampires actually share more genetic similarities with bats than people. And that is why they are similar in many ways. For example, they only come out at night, they both have fangs, they both drink blood and they both have little furry pig faces. Actually, come to think of it, the last one usually only refers to bats. Anyway, vampires and bats are *so* alike that a vampire can **shapeshift** into a bat at will. Being able to turn into a bat means that a vampire can travel large distances in a short space of time and can enter most houses at ease, either by flying through a gap in an open window, or by flying down the chimney. So I'm sorry to inform you of this, girls and boys, but while a chimney is useful for the big guy to come down at Christmas, it is also **lethal** if you have a vampire living nearby! The final thing I can tell you about vampires is that they have no reflection.

So, it is fairly safe to assume that Justin Bieber is not a vampire!

But everyone else — unless you have seen them in the daylight, or you have seen their reflection, be on your guard. They could very well be a vampire!

How to Protect Yourself from a Vampire Attack

So now you better understand what a vampire is, it's time to find out what you can do if you ever come across one. I urge you to take out a pencil and make notes here, because this information is **vital**!

Now I'm not going to lie to you, if you ever come face to face with a vampire then you are in deep doo-doo. But there are things you can do to protect yourself from vampires and help prevent yourself from becoming their next meal!

You've already learned that vampires can turn into bats, which helps them enter your house to feast on your blood, so it makes sense to shut your windows at night. Unfortunately vampires are **crafty**, so it doesn't mean that if you have all your windows bolted you will definitely be sleeping <u>safe and sound</u> in the morning. But closing your windows certainly helps. Leaving your windows open not only allows vampires easy access into your bedroom, it also releases your odour into the air, which can attract nearby vampires.

To vampires, humans are like crisps — we are all flavoured differently. Each blood type gives off a slightly different scent, and while they certainly are not fussy, their favourite flavour is O positive. So if this is your blood type, then closing your windows at night is a must!

But even if you are in the unfortunate position of having O positive blood, there is still something you can do to put a vampire off eating you.

Vampires don't like garlic. It smells utterly **putrid** to them. And, as I'm sure you are aware, if you eat garlic, then you stink of garlic. So if you have had a large helping of garlic recently, then this may be enough to put a vampire off eating you.

Imagine a **scenario** where a vampire breaks into your house and enters the bedroom that you share with a sibling. Well, if you tucked into a chicken kiev for tea, while your brother or sister had fish fingers and chips, then the chances are that the vampire would ignore you and munch on them instead. Result!

But gobbling garlic will only get you so far. If a vampire goes a few days without drinking blood, they become even more **ravenous** than normal. So hungry in fact, that they would still eat you, even if you had eaten garlic for breakfast, lunch and dinner. Think about it. What would you do if you were starving and got a burger from McDonald's but it had a gherkin on top? You would just peel off the slimy critter and eat the burger anyway, right? It may spoil the flavour a bit, but I bet you would still eat it.

At this point I know what you're thinking. You're thinking that all these little tips may help protect you <u>to a degree</u>, but they aren't guaranteed to save you! And you're right. And here is where I have some good news and some bad news for you.

The good news is there are a few ways to kill a vampire.

The bad news is, none of them are easy.

The first thing to be aware of is that vampires cannot go out in the daylight.

Do you know a horrible boy? You may be a horrible boy yourself? Either way, I'm sure you have heard of horrible boys who pour salt onto slugs. When the salt hits the skin of a slug, it causes a chemical reaction that turns their sleek bodies into a mass of sticky ooze. It's disgusting. And it's also **excruciatingly** painful for the slug. Now, when the Ultra Violet rays of the sun hit the skin of a vampire, it has the exact same effect. After just seconds in the sun, a vampire's skin will begin to bubble and smoke, and in no time at all, the creature will turn to dust.

Sadly, this isn't all that helpful. The only way you could kill a vampire this way is by breaking into its house during the daytime, when it is asleep, and pulling open the curtains to let the sunshine blare in. You would then have to prize open the vampire's coffin to expose it to the sunlight. But vampires aren't stupid. They **purposely** sleep in thick coffins that are locked securely from the inside, usually in a room with no windows. So, I would not recommend entering a vampire's house to attempt this, for if you do, you would very likely become their midnight snack (well actually, their midday snack, I suppose).

Probably the best way to destroy a vampire is by soaking them with holy water. When the pure goodness of holy water comes into contact with the evil skin of a vampire, it has a similar effect to sunlight. Even a tiny drop of holy water will cause a bad burn to a vampire and a good soaking will **undoubtedly** lead it to **perish**. You can get holy water in any church. It is in the font by the front door. So keep going, day after day, until you have enough to fill a decent sized bottle and then keep this at your bedside at all times. It may be the wisest thing you will ever do.

So now you are in possession of all of the facts. Chances are you will never need this information as vampires are an extremely rare species. But then you never know, there could be a vampire living on your very street!

Ella's Response

Something strange is happening at Number 33, that's for sure! At least we know what to do now should we suspect a vampire lives nearby. But are we strong enough to survive the bite?

Oh jeepers creepers! I just asked my mum and guess what, my blood type is O positive! EEEEEEK!

I am going to go to the church tomorrow and get some holy water. I am also going to have garlic bread for breakfast and lunch, and garlic chicken for dinner – just to be on the safe side!

My neighbour down the street always has his curtains closed during the day. I saw him digging in his garden one night. His skin was kind of glowing ... should I be worried?

Campaign

Help save our slugs from horrible boys who pour salt on them. Let's do a campaign on why slugs (and snails!) are so important in nature – they may be slimy, but they're very important to have around!

AUTHOR'S INTENT

Why do you think the author wrote this story? What do you think the author is like from reading his work?

135

Story Telling

by Edgar A. Guest

Most every night when they're in bed,
And both their little prayers have said,
They shout for me to come upstairs
And tell them tales of gypsies bold,
And eagles with the claws that hold
A baby's weight, and fairy sprites
That roam the woods on starry nights.

And I must illustrate these tales,
Must imitate the northern gales
That toss the native man's canoe,
And show the way he paddles, too.
If in the story comes a bear,
I have to pause and sniff the air
And show the way he climbs the trees
To steal the honey from the bees.

And then I buzz like angry bees
And sting him on his nose and knees
And howl in pain, till mother cries:
"That pair will never shut their eyes,
While all that noise up there you make;
You're simply keeping them awake."
And then they whisper: "Just one more,"
And once again I'm forced to roar.

New stories every night they ask.
And that is not an easy task;
I have to be so many things,
The frog that croaks, the lark that sings,
The cunning fox, the frightened hen;
But just last night they stumped me, when
They wanted me to twist and squirm
And imitate an angle worm.

At last they tumble off to sleep,
And softly from their room I creep
And brush and comb the shock of hair
I tossed about to be a bear.
Then mother says: "Well, I should say
You're just as much a child as they."
But you can bet I'll not resign
That story telling job of mine.

Narrative

At Work

Tom's Intro

Before the year <u>draws to a close</u>, there is one final story that I wish to share with you. I hope you have enjoyed our adventures this year in *Over the Moon*. Looking forward to seeing you all again soon!

This week we are looking once more at **narrative** texts. Which genre have you enjoyed the most? Let's recap on the ones we have studied: writing to socialise, persuasive, recount, report, explanation, procedural and narrative. Can you remember an example of each?

I have chosen to present to you some text snippets from *Canary in the Coal Mine* by Madelyn Rosenberg. I read this book recently and I couldn't put it down — it is a real page-turner. It links in with the picture book that you are going to study this month, *Town Is by the Sea*. Both stories are about working in the coalmines. What do you think that would be like?

Transfer of skills: There are different birds all over the world. I wonder what the word 'bird' looks like in other languages.

éan (Irish), *uccello* (Italian), *oiseau* (French), *pájaro* (Spanish), *vogel* (German)

Canary in the Coal Mine

(page 1)

Bitty flattened himself against the back of the cage as the Gap-Toothed Man reached his fat hot-dog fingers through the front.

'Here, birdie, birdie,' the man said. 'Come on, birdie. Hurry up, now.' The meaty fingers opened and closed. Bitty **swerved** right, then ducked low. He didn't duck low enough.

'Gotcha.'

(page 2)

'Hope it's a gas,' **hollered** Chester. He was the only one who ever joked about the methane and carbon monoxide that lurked in the mine's dark tunnels.

A half mile later they reached the head frame, the timber structure that housed the mine's elevator, and went in. The Gap-Toothed Man found the lights and pulled the **lever**, sending them down the **shaft**.

(page 3)

'How's the view?' The miner held the cage low to the ground, then close to the ceiling. Bitty swung <u>back and forth</u> again. His feathers were yellow; inside he was green.

(page 5)

The men <u>set up shop</u> in the dark **bowels** of the mine and began hacking away at the vein of coal that ran big and black through Audie Mountain. The Gap-Toothed Man walked among them, making notes and sniffing the air as if he, not Bitty, would be the one to **detect** the gas. The sounds of axes and shovels made conversation tricky. At least there was no blasting today. The canaries' job was simple: breathe and chirp. Stop, and the miners would check for bad air. That was what they called the gas that crept like a ghost through the maze of timber and tunnels.

(page 7)

Canaries were known for making music, but the canaries in the No. 7 rarely went beyond their steady *fee-yo*, like a telegraph repeating the same message in Morse code. They never even sang when they were happy, not that they were happy often, with the exception of Aunt Lou. No, Bitty didn't have <u>a happy place</u>. He had a cold, dark, angry place, and he wanted to get out before they carried him out like Boggs in a matchbox coffin.

The question was how to escape. The **aviary** was locked from the outside with a long metal bar. Bitty couldn't move it. He'd tried. The door opened in the early morning, when it was time for work. It opened at night when Mr. Campbell brought them home again. But the Campbells had <u>quick hands</u>. The door snapped shut in the time it would take to whack a fly.

Bitty tried to think of another way out, but the mine wasn't **conducive** to <u>heavy thinking</u>. Thoughts passed through his brain slowly, as if he had to dig for them. Time passed slowly, too. If there'd been a clock, the hands would have moved backward.

(Page 13)

'Well, it feels like a prison,' Bitty said. He drew himself up to his <u>full height</u>. 'I'm thinking about <u>busting out</u>.'

(Page 15)

Hubert was the only bird who had ever escaped the Big House. He'd done it the **previous** spring, by way of a loose screw on a door hinge. The rest of them had watched as he flew out Jamie's window and into the warmth of a Sunday. There'd been one glorious moment when he'd looked back at them, <u>his face alight</u> with freedom and sunshine. The next moment a dark shadow had swooped over him. A Cooper's hawk. There was a flash of colour as the hawk grabbed Hubert in her talons and squeezed.

(Page 20)

It made him think of 'Gone, Birdie, Gone', a nursery rhyme they'd learned when they were younger:

If the dust don't get you
If the beam don't fall
If the gas don't take you
'Fore the whistle's call

If your breath don't rattle
If your bones don't shake
Then you're gone, birdie, gone
Never more to WAKE!

(Page 69)

Bitty looked up at the night sky and <u>drew in a breath</u>. Back home, he could see only a few stars, shining like cut glass on the small strip of sky that was visible from Jamie's bedroom window. But here? Bitty couldn't even count them all. There must be hundreds. Thousands! He felt as if he could fly up and touch them. He felt as if he could catch them like the summer fireflies that sometimes glowed from a Mason jar on Jamie's nightstand. He wondered if he could see every star in the sky. And he wondered how many of those stars were shining over Coalbank Hollow.

'He may be small, but he dreams big,' Alice joined in the whispered conversation. She looked like springtime herself, with features the colour of mustard flowers.

(Page 85)

'You can't help anybody if you don't get completely well. You just need a <u>plan B</u>.'

Bitty sighed. At the rate he was going, he needed a plan for every letter of the alphabet. He nibbled on a piece of his cinnamon bun, which made him feel a little better. He finally remembered to thank Clarence, which he should have done <u>first thing</u>.

(Page 118)

'I suppose it could be dangerous, if you got caught,' Eck said. 'Nobody in my family has been caught for years.'

Scenery whizzed by. Now Bitty was able to see the country he had missed during his dark, sleepy ride northeast. He could see the mountains stacked behind each other, blue, like waves. The train <u>snaked along</u> beside them and through them, passing towns and valleys and gaps. At each station, the train paused just long enough for a hiccup. As they approached Oak Hill, Clarence's mother **bobbed** her head at them. 'Be careful, now, all of you,' she said. 'Remember, our aunt Zelda is your aunt Zelda. You know where to find me! Oh, dear, I'd better hurry before I —' A flutter of feathers, and she was gone.

(Page 123)

'Where would we sleep?' asked Chester.

'Trees,' Bitty said. 'We'll build nests. Really comfortable nests with cotton and straw and leaves.'

The free birds set up a camp tucked away in the green needles of a cedar tree, while the rest of the canaries stayed crowded in the Big House. Uncle Aubrey was more like a lion than a bird; he roared whenever anybody tried to talk to him. Clarence had <u>a hard time</u> being out of work, too. The miners were gone all day, and the women walked too quickly from one thing to the next. Clarence tried following Mrs. Campbell around, but she almost kicked him twice when she hung out the laundry. He was forced to eat berries instead of bread.

(Page 133)

'This is it,' Bitty announced. 'My last night in a cage.'

In the near distance, the church bells rang, celebration and sorrow clanging <u>in harmony</u>. When they stopped ringing, Bo Collins cleared his throat and wiped sweat from his forehead.

'There's five that <u>didn't make it</u>,' he said.

Uncle Aubrey counted; that meant they'd saved one, two – seven humans, counting Jamie. Even more if you counted the rescue crew. But five lives lost. No one made a sound as the foreman announced the names of <u>the fallen men</u>. Bitty knew all of them. One name he knew better than the others: Hurley, Steven J. The Gap-Toothed Man.

(Page 138)

For they were so brave that they risked their lives to save the lives of men.

'I don't know about you guys, but I wasn't brave,' Chester said. 'I was scared <u>out of my mind</u>.'

It was the first time Bitty could remember Chester admitting he was afraid.

'I just figured something out,' Bitty said. 'Being brave doesn't mean you're not scared. It means you keep on going when you are.'

Chester thought about that. 'So what you're saying is that if I was *more* scared than the rest of you, that means I was the bravest one. Right?'

'We were *all* brave,' Bitty said. His heart <u>swelled with pride</u> even as the September wind **ruffled** his feathers. Soon they would have to leave this place.

'We'll <u>catch a chill</u> if we stay much longer,' said Aunt Lou, echoing his thoughts. She perched above him, on the miner's solid shoulder. 'But we'll come back. I'm sure we'll come back.'

'A chill?' said Uncle Aubrey, who was **perched** on the miner's boot. 'We have to get moving. We can't risk a chill. Think of what that could do to our voices! Our voices are our livelihoods.'

Bitty smiled and shook his head. *Some things never change*, he thought. *But others …*

He stood on the tips of his toes and stretched his wings as far as they could go. He didn't hit Chester. Or a perch. Or a metal bar. He didn't hit anything but the crisp September air. He felt like flying.

'Come on,' he said to Alice and Chester. 'Let's go.'

'Where are we going this time?' they asked <u>in unison</u>.

Bitty looked at the clouds which were parting now, their **grieving** done. He looked at the blue West Virginia sky.

'Up,' he said.

TOM'S RESPONSE

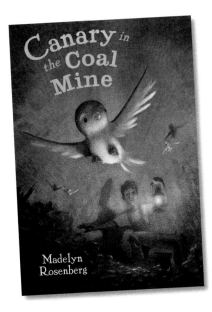

Canary in the Coal Mine

Madelyn Rosenberg

I told you it was a page-turner! The suspense was killing me! Can you predict what happened in the rest of the story?

What do you think of the front cover? If you had to design a front cover, what would it look like?

Why did the miners need the birds?

What was it like for the miners working in the mine?

How is this story similar to *The One and Only Ivan*?

Poll Did Bitty get out: Yes or No?

What would happen if Bitty got caught trying to bust out?

How would Bitty get out of there without being noticed?

Clap the beat to the song.

If the dust don't get you
If the beam don't fall
If the gas don't take you
'Fore the whistle's call
If your breath don't rattle
If your bones don't shake
Then you're gone, birdie, gone
Never more to WAKE!

Author's Intent

Why do you think the author wrote this book?

The Owl and the Pussy-Cat

by Edward Lear

I

The Owl and the Pussy-cat went to sea
   In a beautiful pea-green boat,
They took some honey, and plenty of money,
   Wrapped up in a five-pound note.
The Owl looked up to the stars above,
   And sang to a small guitar,
'O lovely Pussy! o Pussy, my love,
   What a beautiful Pussy you are,
   You are,
   You are!
What a beautiful Pussy you are!'

II

Pussy said to the Owl, 'You elegant fowl!
   How charmingly sweet you sing!
O let us be married! Too long we have tarried:
   But what shall we do for a ring?'
They sailed away, for a year and a day,
   To the land where the Bong-tree grows
And there in a wood a Piggy-wig stood
   With a ring at the end of his nose,
   His nose,
   His nose,
With a ring at the end of his nose.

III

'Dear Pig, are you willing to sell for one shilling
   Your ring?' Said the Piggy, 'I will'.
So they took it away, and were married next day
   By the Turkey who lives on the hill.
They dined on mince, and slices of quince,
   Which they ate with a runcible spoon;
And hand in hand, on the edge of the sand,
   They danced by the light of the moon,
   The moon,
   The moon,
They danced by the light of the moon.

GOOD READERS

Have a purpose for reading.

Look at pictures when possible.

Practise.

Think about what they already know.

Predict what will happen next.

Try to figure out new words.

Make sure they understand what they read.

Draw conclusions about what they read.

Form pictures in their minds.

Good readers read every day.

Word Attack Strategies

Flip the sound

a
e
i
o
u
c
g
oo
ow
_y

Cross-check

Did the word you said
look right?
sound right?
make sense?

Rhyming robot

proud

reminds me of loud
and cloud

Chunky monkey

Look for chunks
you know.

be-ing
yes-ter-day

Cover the ending

wanted

Cover the -ed to
focus on the base
word 'want'. Then
add the -ed back.

Use the pictures

'Oh, that word must
be "castle" since I see
one in the picture.'

Skip the word

Read the rest of the
sentence, then come
back and try again.

Sometimes there are
clues in the sentence
that can help
you figure
it out.

3 sounds of -ed

/t/ baked

/d/ waved

/d/ haunted

When two vowels go walking ...

'e'

meat

... the first one
does the talking.

Magic e

'u'

cube

She makes the vowel
say its name but she
stays silent.

Reading Comprehension Strategies

	Predicting	Share your prediction about what you think the text will be about: I think ..., I predict ..., I anticipate ...
	Clarifying	Invite members of the group to clarify anything that is unclear: tricky words, locations, purpose of the text, text type ...
	Visualising	Invite members of the group to share the mental images they made while reading. How were your mental images similar or different?
	Connection **text-to-text** **text-to-world** **text-to-self**	Invite members of the group to make connections to other books, texts, movies or events: This reminds me of ... I remember when ...
	Questioning	Invite members of the group to ask a who, what, where, when, why or how question about the text.
	Summarising	Summarise what the text was about. Invite members of the group to make a different summary or to add to yours.

Literary Genres

Mystery

A suspenseful story about a puzzling event that is not solved until the end of the story.

Historical Fiction

A fictional story that takes place in a specific time period; often the setting is real, but the characters are made up.

Fantasy

A story that is not possible and may include talking animals or magical powers.

Traditional Literature

Stories that are passed down from one group to another (includes fairy tales, folk tales, myths, fables and legends).

Science Fiction

A type of fantasy that uses science and technology (robots, time travel, machines).

Informational

Texts that provide facts about a variety of topics.

Realistic Fiction

A story that uses fictional characters, but could happen.

Autobiography

The story of a real person's life that is written by that person.

Biography

The story of a real person's life that is written by another person.

Poetry

Verse written to create a response of thought and feeling from the reader; it often uses rhythm and rhyme.